STRATEGIES
FOR EDUCATING
AFRICAN AMERICAN
ADULTS

OTHER BOOKS FROM UMI

Leaders' guides are also available for teaching these
subjects in midweek Bible studies, adult and young adult
Sunday Schools, church retreats, and training hours.

STRATEGIES FOR EDUCATING AFRICAN AMERICAN ADULTS

ALVIN LEWIS, PH.D.

Urban Ministries, Inc.

CHICAGO, ILLINOIS

Strategies for Educating African American Adults

Publisher

UMI
(Urban Ministries, Inc.)
P.O. Box 436987
Chicago, IL 60643-6987
1-800-860-8642
www.urbanministries.com

First Edition
First Printing

Library of Congress Cataloging-in-Publication Data

Strategies for Educating African American Adults/Alvin Lewis, Ph.D.
Includes bibliographic references
ISBN 1-932715-80-0
ISBN 978-1-932715-80-4

1. Education. 2. Multicultural education 3. Christian education

Library of Congress Control Number: 2006932113

Printed in the United States of America.

DEDICATION

This book is dedicated to my wife of 46 years, Juanita Lewis, Ph.D., M.S.W., whose love and loyalty have remained steadfast and whose patience and understanding have been enduring. She has served with me for nearly five decades with distinction and dedication. I thank God daily for the love and experiences we have shared over the years.

I also dedicate this book to my mother, Lillie Mae Lewis, who went home to be with the Lord in February 2005. My mother has been a good role model and constant source of encouragement in more ways than I am able to enumerate. She instilled in me a passion for the pursuit of knowledge and a belief in the God of the Bible. Even at age 96, she still had a keen intellect and could engage people in stimulating conversation.

I want to pay special tribute to my Aunt Lucile Gant, who also went home to be with the Lord in October 2003. Aunt Lu, as she was affectionately called, was like a second mother to me. Through her knowledge of the Bible she developed unique gifts and skills as a Sunday School teacher, communicator, lay Bible scholar, and as an example of the Spirit of Christ in her daily living. I greatly miss her.

ACKNOWLEDGMENTS

Over the years, I have met many wonderful people who have made significant contributions to my life. In writing this book, I have had to draw from the research and writings of many authors, whose works have enhanced this book in a significant number of ways.

My special gratitude to Dr. Donald Courtney, now deceased, whose encouragement, trust, and tutelage prompted me to write while I was a staff member on the Board of Christian Education, Church of God, from 1974–1989. As Executive Director, Don insisted that all Christian Education staff members should engage in creative and productive writing assignments.

A personal word of appreciation goes to Dr. James Earl Massey, Christian mentor, scholar, author, preacher, and Dean Emeritus, Anderson University, School of Theology. His careful reading and critiquing of the manuscript, with suggested improvements, enhanced the quality of this book. I am also grateful to Dr. Massey for writing an insightful foreword to this book. Dr. Massey's encouragement and support is gratefully received not only for his words of inspiration but also for his example of discipline and excellence in scholarship.

Special thanks goes to Dr. Kenneth Hall, former Director of Curriculum for Warner Press, Church of God in Anderson, Indiana, for permission to adapt his non-published article on *Relational Teaching*. Generous appreciation is also extended to all of the former staff members with whom I served on the Board of Christian Education, Church of God, Anderson, Indiana: Rev. Kenneth Prunty, Rev. Dale Senseman, and Dr. Joseph Cookston, and for the materials they helped to produce in chapters 13–16. A hearty thanks goes to Arthur Kelly of Congregational Ministries for giving permission to utilize some of the charts and articles from previous writings of the annual Sunday School *Resource Packets* from 1982–1990.

Dr. Bennie Goodwin rendered invaluable assistance by making many helpful suggestions to the original manuscript. His careful review and wise advice was of immeasurable value in strengthening this book.

Finally, I owe a debt of gratitude for the excellent input and contribution made to this manuscript by my wife, Juanita Lewis, Ph.D. Over the years, she has been my partner in ministry and has called forth the best gifts from my life. She has always believed in me, even when I may have doubted myself. Truly, she has been the "wind beneath my wings." She also sacrificially performed the Herculean task of typing the original manuscript, and served as proofreader and advisor of this project. Without her watchful eye, attention to details, and earnest devotion, it is doubtful if this book would have been completed.

Believe me when I say that any shortcomings, omissions, or inadvertent exclusions in this book are strictly from my head and not from my heart. I have assumed the blame for what *should have been, could have been, and would have been* included in a book of this type.

Alvin Lewis, Ph.D., M.Div.

Jackson, Mississippi

CONTENTS

FOREWORD

This book is a creative, much needed, and timely contribution to the spiritual health and development of the Black church. Its author, Dr. Alvin Lewis, has aptly demonstrated an understanding of the goals of Christian education for the African American setting, and he has set forth in clear terms a process to guide pastors and others in reaching those life-enriching goals.

The process Dr. Lewis has set forth takes into account the unique social background of the African American family and the particular needs of the church seeking to minister to that family. The goals enumerated in this book have not been projected apart from the history, social setting, and needs of African Americans.

Dr. Lewis has written from the perspective of an educator, intent to inform, but his book is something other than mere theory or an armchair statement. He has prepared this work after many years of teaching, writing, pastoring, and serving as an administrator in the field this book reflects. The selection and development of the topics treated here grew out of experience and research within several churches and across several years of ministry.

Strategies for Educating African American Adults presents an essential teaching-learning process with spiritual and practical outcomes for the African American family and church.

This book by Dr. Lewis rightfully takes its place within a steadily growing list of resources for the Black church, but it deserves a high place in the list because of the specific guidance it grants to those families and churches eager to attain the ends it projects *for* them and, ultimately, *through* them to others.

James Earl Massey
Dean Emeritus,
Anderson University School of Theology

INTRODUCTION

Strategies for Educating African American Adults is about teaching, learning, and leading in African American churches. My hope is that the content would be viewed as a comprehensive resource to guide those who plan, teach, and administer Christian education in local churches. Besides addressing the Christian education needs in African American churches, this book will also find wide appeal for all Christian educators. This book is presented in six motivating and challenging parts.

Part one begins with an overview of the conditions that most African Americans had to endure during the period of slavery, along with the experiences of institutional and personal racism that followed. Chapter one is followed up by chapter two's brief exposition on the heritage and future of Christian education in the Black church.

Part two provides the reader with a review of characteristics of young, middle, and older adult learners, referred to as the Buster, Boomer, and Builder generations.

The *what* and *how* of teaching adults are explored in part three. You'll find some interesting and exciting teaching principles as well as suggested programs in this section.

Part four looks at some of the challenges of ministering to families. It acknowledges serious problems among African American families, then suggests specific classes for couples before and after marriage, as well as for parents and married children, along with seminars in communication skills.

The Sunday School in African American churches is the focus of part five. In this section you'll discover 17 practical and easy-to-follow ways to enliven, increase, and enhance this premier Christian education organization.

Values—core and Christian—are the topics of part six. How are values described and defined? How are they to be understood, developed, and committed to? And how are values positively related to the church and its ministry of Christian education? These are some of the questions raised and addressed in this part of the book.

Strategies for Educating African American Adults closes with an extensive resource section. This appendix is a guide to a great deal of helpful knowledge for those interested in adult Christian education in the Black church.

And now it is time to begin exploring the fascinating field of adult Christian education. And remember, if knowledge is power, then knowledge anointed and disciplined by the Holy Spirit provides teachers, learners, and leaders with divine power!

PART I:

A LOOK
AT THE PAST
AND THE FUTURE

CHAPTER 1

HISTORICAL BACKGROUND AND BEGINNINGS

The journey of Black people in America has taken many paths, and the directions of these paths have been far different from those of their White counterparts. The period of slavery, and the years that followed, left countless scars on the collective psyche of Black people in America. We must take this into account as we consider Christian education for African Americans.

Joseph V. Crockett has written, "For Christian Education to be effective in African-American experiences, it must have cultural integrity with the African-American experiences and traditions."[1] Crockett further maintains that to keep integrity with teaching and learning in an African American cultural, biblical, and historical context, we must understand the following:

> African Americans have a heritage rich with the rhythms of heroines and heroes. We have a soul born in the bosom of African soil that has laughed through the labor pains of injustice and sung through the sin of slavery. Our communities are stitched with the threads of deferred dreams and realized hope. We are made with the fabric of struggle for a purpose-filled existence, while striving to be true to ourselves, our ancestry and our native land.[2]

I might add, we are also striving to be true to our God as we seek to rediscover our noble historical foundation.

OUR AFRICAN BIBLICAL ROOTS

Teaching and learning in an African American church setting must address a broad spectrum of our Black history and heritage. Although it is true that this book seeks to address primarily the African church in America, the history and heritage of African people certainly far exceeds their lives in America and Europe.

To leave out our rich African biblical heritage in both Old and New Testaments would be to dishonor the true identity of our Christian faith. Therefore, for teaching and learning to be effective in the African American church, we should make an attempt to connect our ancient biblical past to our present-day reality.

Dr. Charles B. Copher, former distinguished professor of Old Testament at the Interdenominational Theological Center in Atlanta, Georgia, illustrates the connection of African Americans to their biblical past. According to Copher,

> Africa figures prominently in the biblical history from earliest times of creation, when according to the biblical account four rivers went out from the Garden of Eden, one of which was the Gihon River which went around the whole land of Cush or Ethiopia—a river that many view as the River Nile.... Africa figures again in the initial peopling of the earth as indicated in the Table of Nations recorded in Genesis 10:6–10 and 1 Chronicles 1:8–16. There are three African Nations (Cush/Ethiopia, Mizrain/Egypt ...and Put [Phut]/Libya) and their offspring are referred to.[3]

Dr. Copher further states, "A black presence in the Old Testament may be firmly established. Such a presence is attested in many passages and in many ways, from earliest times to the period of restoration. It appears in literature from many periods of Old Testament history, in historical accounts and in prophetic oracles; in the Psalms and in the literature of love, the Song of Songs."[4]

Other connections that relate to our African heritage reveal the following Bible truths:

1. Africa was once called Ham (Psalm 68:31; Matthew 2:13–15).
2. The world's first empire after the Flood was founded and ruled by Ham's grandson Nimrod (Genesis 10:8–10).

3. The country now known as Ethiopia is first mentioned in Genesis 2:13.

4. The geographical region known as the Holy Land, Canaan, or the land of milk and honey was inhabited and governed by Black people of the lineage of Ham (Genesis 9:18; 10:15–19; 12:5–6; Exodus 3:8).

Apparently Black people played an important role in the early Christian church as well. "Now in the church that was at Antioch there were certain prophets and teachers: Barnabas, Simeon who was called Niger, Lucius of Cyrene [North Africa], Manaen who had been brought up with Herod the Tetrarch, and Saul. As they ministered to the Lord and fasted, the Holy Spirit said, 'Now separate to Me Barnabas and Saul for the work to which I have called them'" (Acts 13:1–3, NKJV). This passage is significant because it links the prophetic and teaching ministry to three Black Christian personalities—Simeon, Lucius, and Manaen—who had a vital role in shaping early Christianity.

In an insightful comment concerning the value of identifying Black people in Scripture, Rev. Walter McCray writes,

> The student who searches the Scripture will find that Black peoples were genuine and pertinent members of the Biblical community of faith. In fact, the Old Testament community of faith was basically Black in its roots. Black people lived under both the Old and New Covenants. Their presence and importance were not inflated, or negated. . . . It is therefore important, especially for African Americans, to appreciate the Black presence in the Scripture.[5]

Therefore, when Black people are taught and nurtured from the Bible, should they not expect to be endowed with a more mature knowledge and practical wisdom to understand their own biblical and cultural legacy? Shouldn't Black congregations in America strongly promote an Afro-centric point of view, which is a concept rooted in the collective consciousness and experiences of Black people throughout the world? At the same time, shouldn't we endeavor to promote the contributions, history, and culture of African people wherever they are found?

Dr. Cain Hope Felder, professor at Howard Divinity School in Washington, D.C., writes, "The major news story is not that there are Blacks in the Bible. The major news story has to do with the wonderful inclusiveness of ancient biblical cultures where all people are seen as worthy of doing remarkable things when their story is told and identified with the power of God."[6]

We should not measure greatness just by European/American or Asian standards; rather, we should view Africa as a place where greatness also originated and spread to many other cultures and nations.

AN AFRO-CENTRIC PERSPECTIVE

We should celebrate and extol the virtues of Black people, both ancient and contemporary, who have contributed in meaningful ways to the lives of all people. At the same time, we need to construct new models and paradigms of teaching, learning, and leading African American people to help build more positive relationships, stronger families, better churches, and a healthier self-esteem.

In no way does an Afro-centric point of view seek to denigrate European, American, or other ethnic contributions. Instead, the Afro-centric concept strives to reveal the effects of hundreds of years of neglect, due to racism, miseducation, and the cultural fleecing of Black people.

Anthony Browder provides a balanced prospective with regard to an Afro-centric position. He states,

> We must be very mindful of the fact that just one hundred and fifty years ago, African Americans were still slaves. By law, we were forbidden from learning [by society and church] to read and write. The reasons were very obvious. Information is power. Information holds the key to freedom from mental and physical bondage.... If you deny any people the knowledge of their history and culture, you deny them the ability to develop to their full potential. It is the responsibility of every adult to know their history and culture, to preserve it and to pass it on to the next generation.[7]

Browder's words are instructive for African Americans who have embraced the Christian religion as a lifestyle and worldview. It becomes even more instructive to our way of life when we consider that culture is the foundation and principal agent through which societies convey their beliefs and norms. Our religious views also hold the experiences of a community in its customs, rituals, and mores.

In his book *Primitive Culture,* Edward B. Taylor summarizes how culture has a far-reaching impact on individuals and their development: "Culture or civilization, taken in its wide ethnographic sense, is that complex whole which includes knowledge, belief, art, morals, law, custom, and any other capabilities and habits acquired by [persons] who are members of society."[8]

For Christian education to be relevant and culturally specific to African Americans, it must intentionally promote holistic growth. Other aspects should include evaluation of the Christian faith and a relational quality of life that inspires unity, harmony, and love. Finally, we need to embrace a lifestyle guided by the Word of God and empowered by the Holy Spirit.

CHAPTER 2

THE ROLE OF THE AFRICAN AMERICAN CHURCH IN CHRISTIAN EDUCATION

In their study *The Black Church in the African American Experience,* C. Eric Lincoln and Lawrence H. Mamiya explain the critical role that the African American church plays in shaping and promoting Christian education. In their study of nearly 2,000 Black congregations and pastors, the authors write the following about Black history:

> Despite the fact that teaching slaves to read and write was against the law, slaves had a persistent desire to be educated. Many slaves saw reading as a means of helping them to read the Bible and enlarging [their] opportunities to broader dimensions of education. The slaves who learned to read and write were often looked upon as leaders and teachers in the slave community.[1]

RELIGIOUS CENTERS OF BLACK EDUCATION

After the end of slavery, Black people continued to pursue Christian education within their churches as well as in other social environments. These attempts produced many influential options for the education of African Americans down to our own day.

The Sunday School. One of the first places Black people made contact with the educational process was the Sunday School. First hearing and memorizing spoken

Scriptures from the Bible, they eventually learned how to read the Bible for themselves. This was a great achievement for a substantial number of newly emancipated slaves.

Black Colleges. In addition to the Sunday School, there were other educational efforts made through Black churches to lift the social, moral, and spiritual standards of African Americans. Through the Freedman's Bureau, white philanthropists, missionary societies, and individual Black churches, schools were established that emphasized religious and moral education.

Several Black churches were instrumental in giving birth to now well-known Black colleges and universities. These schools were often housed in the basements of Black churches or in small buildings erected on land donated by these churches. Morehouse University in Atlanta, for example, can trace its history to a school founded in 1866 in the basement of Springfield Baptist Church in Augusta, Georgia. Friendship Baptist Church was influential in giving birth to Spelman College in Atlanta. Tuskegee University (formally Tuskegee Institute) had its origin in the basement of Butler Chapel A.M.E. Zion Church in Tuskegee, Alabama.

Black Denominations. Numerous Black denominational bodies established their own colleges and seminaries. The importance of these denominations to both secular and religious education has been their genius in inspiring African Americans to live a better quality of life socially, spiritually, and educationally. As far back as 1896, at a Quadrennial of the African Methodist Episcopal Church, the bishops presented a list of educational and social concerns to those in attendance. Some of the items mentioned were the following:

1. To give an opportunity to show by example what is possible for the Negro to do for himself.
2. To stand as a living protest against caste in the church at the Sacramental table and in the ministry.
3. To increase in young men and women Race Pride
   - By preserving the biographies of great men [and women] of the [African] race.
   - By showing that we need not be ashamed of our origin and ancestry.

- By showing that originally the Negroes were the leaders of civilizations.
- By documenting that Black people were among the most active promoters of Christianity.[2]

THE STRUGGLE FOR LIBERATION

The growth and development of Christian education in the Black church in America has been evolutionary. As social, political, and racial issues have pushed to the forefront of the African American struggle, there has been a corresponding effort to shape a Christian education curriculum to address these pressing concerns.

In the Black church (as with most people caught in the struggle of racial and social injustice), Christian education has taken on a practical and liberational tone. The center of discussion in Bible studies, whether in Sunday School or in other educational settings, often focuses on themes of family, economics, race, and justice. Although these concerns are not exclusive to African Americans, they have shaped our history, heritage, and Christian faith.

Given the unique historical and social situations of Black people in America, Christian education has taken a backseat to preaching, singing, and praying in Black churches. In many Black churches preaching, and not teaching, has been the primary means of educating the masses. The largest attendance in most Black churches takes place at the Sunday morning worship service, with only a faithful few adults attending Sunday School.

If teaching and learning is to flourish in our African American churches, we must utilize the Sunday experiences and other occasions for greater emphasis upon educating our people. Rather than trying to pack all of our Christian education into the Sunday School hour, we can utilize other days of the week and the weekends to carry out educational ministries.

James Harris points out,

> In the black church, Christian Education has to be about freedom and liberation. Consequently, teaching people to read and study, to respect themselves and others, and to practice love and peace in the context of

the black community will lead to what Paulo Freire calls "educating for critical consciousness." Black theology is the paradigm for teaching black Christians how to practice the teachings of Jesus and the prophets. In fact, the black church should be the key factor to bring about liberation, transformation and change.[3]

Christian education in Black churches is thus a process of teaching people how to live and love as Christ taught us to do. It is learning how to apply to all facets of our lives the biblical message and principles enunciated by Christ. And so, if Christian education is to be most effective, it must permeate every facet in the life of each Christian teacher and learner.

ENRICHING CHRISTIAN EDUCATION

Black churches can become more creative and intentional in their approach to teaching adults and helping them learn. We can develop new models and new ways of doing Christian education. Although the Sunday School has been our primary means of presenting and promoting education for adults, there are now congregations that have taken Christian education to newer and higher levels.

Some churches have found Wednesday nights to be a time of extending learning beyond the traditional Bible study and prayer service. Many of these congregations conduct five or more different classes concurrently on Wednesday nights. Topics cover a broad range of interests and needs. Some of the subjects addressed in these sessions deal with marriage, child rearing, money management, and conflict resolution. Basic literacy programs help adults develop reading and writing skills.

In some church bulletins it is not rare to see a list of classes on such subjects as computer training, music reading, piano lessons for adults, parent education, and teaching leadership development to adults and children. In addition, there are classes on leadership for ministers, deacons, trustees, superintendents, mission workers, and leaders of men's and women's organizations.

The Black church must be courageous enough to teach the "whole counsel of God." A sound Christian education program enables adults to gain knowledge about the Bible and how to conquer many of the social and spiritual problems they encounter. Christian teaching and learning in the Black church can emphasize freedom, justice, and living in right relationships as brothers and sisters in the church, the home, and the world.

To engage in this kind of creative Christian education requires rethinking the way we teach and what we teach. We may need to review, reinvent, and rewrite the curriculum materials handed down to us. New approaches and methods may require teachers to seek training on how to teach adult learners.

Over the years, I have observed that teachers teach adults in the same way they teach children. Shouldn't there be more respect for what adults bring into the learning environment from their experiences, knowledge, and expertise? Too often, adult teachers pose questions to the learner, then proceed to answer the questions themselves. On the other hand, when proper preparation is given to the topic by the adult teacher and learner—coupled with an open atmosphere to liberally explore the topic—real, dynamic learning may occur.

EFFECTIVE TEACHING

Teaching at its best is spiritually challenging and engages the mind and spirit of both the teacher and the learner. The drama of learning is best experienced when both the teacher and learner can come away from the session with positive feelings, knowing that discovery and enlightenment have transpired. The teaching-learning process in this case is an interaction among the teacher, the learner, and God.

God requires that all His children—teachers and learners—be open to His divine truth revealed in the Bible. As we open ourselves to the Holy Spirit, He will lead and guide us into all truth (John 16:13).

Teaching and learning in African American churches in the twenty-first century can be expected to assume an aggressive posture that will include some of the following concepts regarding adult Christian education:

1. Educational programs and experiences that are geared toward liberation themes and the struggles of Black people
2. The recruitment of Black writers who are conversant with the historical and daily problems faced by Black people

3. Teachers trained to teach Black adults at the different stages of adult development—young adulthood, middle adulthood, and older adulthood
4. Black churches, along with Black pastoral leadership, actively involved in cyber and virtual technology as a way to help teachers teach more effectively

To ensure the legacy of teaching and learning in our African American churches, it is imperative that educational opportunities are provided for lay teachers, Sunday School superintendents, directors of Christian education, and members of Christian education boards. This continuing education effort can be carried out through workshops, conferences, and seminars.

PART II:

A DESCRIPTION
OF THREE
GENERATIONS

A DESCRIPTION
OF THREE GENERATIONS

Many terms may be used to describe adults in different age groups. Those born between 1965 and 1983 are known as Busters; those born between 1946 and 1964 are called Boomers; and senior adults born between 1927 and 1945 are called Builders. Other names used to describe Busters are the following: Generation X, Millennials, and the Me Generation. Boomers are also known as Beatniks, Yuppies, and Post-War Babies. Older adults are sometimes called the GI Generation, the Silent Generation, and Seniors.

The old expression "one size fits all" certainly does not apply when it is viewed within the context of teaching and planning Christian education initiatives for adults. As noted above, adults cover a broad age span and their unique experiences must be taken into consideration with regard to changing needs throughout the family life cycle. Educational programs must be tailored for each adult generation with respect to personal interests, felt needs, values, and priorities. The following chart provides a breakdown of four generations of adults.

Adult Generations	Born Between	Other Titles
Busters	1965-1983	Generation X Millennials Me Generation
Boomers	1946-1964	Beatniks Yuppies Post-war Babies
Builders	1927-1945	Older Adults GI Generation Silent Generation Seniors
Older Seniors	Before 1927	Older Seniors

There are also a couple of other adult generations alive at this time. Those persons born in 1926 and earlier are considered older seniors. And then there are the Bridgers, who are so named because their birth years span two centuries. They were born between 1980 and 2000 are and just beginning to rise in numbers among America's adult population.

In this section, I concentrate primarily on the Busters, Boomers, and Builders. Here are some of the differences among these groups that Gary McIntosh points out in his book *One Church, Four Generations*.[1]

Busters' values and beliefs were shaped by the 1980s, 1990s, and 2000s. They have been influenced by Roe v. Wade, high technology, video games, high-definition television, space exploration, a broad range of music (rap, rock, rhythm and blues), the Persian Gulf War, and the present administration. Busters are interested in freedom, community causes, and practical education and tend to postpone marriage.

The values and philosophy of Boomers were developed by the decades of the 1950s, 1960s, and 1970s. They witnessed the Cold War, television, economic affluence, education, and technology as well as rock 'n' roll, various assassinations, the space race, the Vietnam War, the energy crisis, and Watergate, including the resignation of President Richard M. Nixon. Boomers tend to be well educated, media oriented, and independent and to be supporters of social causes. They want to live out their faith but to question authority. They are on a spiritual pilgrimage and enjoy learning and sharing in small groups.

The principles, philosophy, and values of Builders were hewed out by the decades of the 1920s, 1930s, and 1940s. The Builder generation saw the Great Depression, World War II, the Roaring Twenties, and the transition from a rural to urban lifestyle. They also witnessed the emergence of the automobile industry, the big bands, and the New Deal. These events, along with the mass media and federal, state, and local legislation, have impacted the Builder's family, church, and school. Builders are far more conservative in their values and faith than are younger folks. As a whole, they are hard workers and frugal savers and are patriotic, private, dependable, and intolerant. They also have a greater commitment to the church, enjoy Bible study, worship out of duty, and attend Sunday School.

Many adult Sunday School classes and teaching situations encompass a broad range of age differences, experiences, needs, and life orientations. All adults were not created to be, nor are meant to be, equal. In the following chapters, let's meet and get to know some adults who bring to the learning situation a variety of concerns, developmental experiences, and perspectives about life.

CHAPTER 3

THE YOUNG ADULT YEARS—THE BUSTER GENERATION

Mary is 25 years old, single, and Black. She is working on a graduate degree in social work and has decided to postpone marriage until she earns her degree. She is dating Tom, who is 28 and a graduate student in engineering at a nearby university. Mary and Tom have been dating for two years but have had no serious discussion about marriage, though each has certainly thought about it. On rare occasions they have hinted about it in a subdued fashion.

Both Mary and Tom are members of a young adult Sunday School class as well as a college-age group that meets periodically for fellowship, food, and Bible study. Like many other young African American adults, they struggle with spiritual, moral, racial, and other critical issues demanding sensible biblical solutions.

Those who teach the age group to which Mary and Tom belong should consider that many young adults are still in the formative stages of career development and are making a number of other adjustments as well. Christian education among African Americans in this age group needs to take into account their particular situation and respond appropriately.

YOUNG ADULT DEVELOPMENT

Some young adults may be entering college or graduate school, while others may be finishing college and are ready to enter the world of work. Some of the pressing life experiences they face are getting married, living apart from parents, and moving to a new area where family members may not be accessible to them. And these major life changes might be just the start of what they are going through, not always smoothly.

As a college teacher, I had the opportunity to observe many young Black (and White) adults whose parents and/or churches thought they had prepared them for the real world. A majority of those young adults, although church members, often made poor decisions when confronted with moral choices and personal responsibilities. Some found themselves in a college environment where they had to make independent decisions about things they were unaccustomed to. A considerable number of them failed or did poorly academically. Some engaged in too many parties while trying to make adjustments in their freshman and sophomore years. Countless other young adults were sent home because of unacceptable conduct or an unplanned pregnancy.

In no way do I want to paint a bleak picture of all African American college students. To be sure, there are many successful young adults who have made great strides during their college pursuits.

At the same time, college is only one setting where young adults may be found. A significant number of young adults don't go to college but do get married, have children, begin new careers, and travel to new places. A few remain home with their parents because they are unemployed or, perhaps, are seeking employment. Like their counterparts in the nation's universities, these young adults are navigating the tricky waters of their stage in life.

In his historic work *Human Development and Education*, R. J. Havighurst, former professor at the University of Chicago, lists eight developmental tasks of early adulthood:

1.   Selecting a mate
2.   Learning to live with a marriage partner
3.   Starting a family
4.   Rearing children
5.   Managing a home
6.   Getting started in an occupation

7. Taking on [social] responsibilities
8. Finding a congenial social group[1]

These developmental tasks apply to most young adults without regard to ethnic or cultural orientation. For a large group of young Black adults, however, there are the added dangers of crack cocaine, crime-infested neighborhoods, single-parent families, and abject poverty.

Young adulthood is often a transition process of liberating oneself from one's birth family and moving into a more autonomous living arrangement. Finding one's place in society and establishing an identity apart from one's nuclear and extended family is sometimes crucial to an ability to make mature and independent decisions.

The Black church can play a crucial role in young adults' lives by planning educational experiences that treat the issues that are on their hearts and meet their particular needs.

TEACHING
YOUNG ADULTS

Every church should do an in-house evaluation of the adults who make up their congregation. They should survey the needs of those adults, with a special focus on separating the concerns of young, middle, and older adults. Meanwhile, however, I would like to suggest several classes with broad appeal for young adults between the ages of 18 and 34.

When considering study topics, we need to remember that young adulthood is filled with a variety of teachable moments. A teachable moment occurs when a life experience intersects with a person's inability to cope with a crisis. One such teachable moment occurs when a person leaves the comfort and security of a stable home and discovers that being on his or her own is not all this young adult assumed it was. For the church, teachable moments are great opportunities.

If you are a teacher of young African American adults, listed below are some of the topics that can be covered in your Christian education classes for them. Each of these classes can help turn young adult challenges into teachable moments that lead to greater Christlikeness.

1. "Leaving Home with a Good Attitude"

This class or workshop could help young adults deal with living independent of parents and family; learn how to manage money, time, and relationships; make wise choices; and practice keeping in touch with parents and family.

2. "How to Get Along with Parents While Living in Their Home"

Difficulties can easily ensue for families when adult children live with parents and yet want to live by their own rules. A conference and/or workshop could focus on respect, responsibility, authority, boundaries, anger, conflict, and giving and receiving love.

3. "Help for Single Parents"

This class could serve a broad range of singles. For example, separate classes could be held for single fathers and single mothers. Some could also be geared to issues facing divorced or separated parents or grandparents who are raising grandchildren alone. Some of the topics may include the following:

- Bible principles for child rearing
- How to handle a strong-willed child
- Extending parental responsibility to other family members
- How children develop
- Communication skills between parents and children

4. "So You Want to Get Married"

In this class, discussion and class assignments could center on such topics as marriage readiness, educational preparation, mental and emotional preparation, family histories, money management, attitudes about sexuality, and marital communication.

5. "How to Get a Job and Keep It"

Sometime in their lives, most adults have lost a job due to their own neglect and ineptitude. At the same time, adults often purposely change their jobs and careers, seeking larger salaries and better benefits. Therefore, a class or workshop could prove beneficial to young adults dealing with topics such as these: handling job applications, résumés, and interviews; getting to work on time; developing a good work ethic; keeping a positive attitude toward coworkers; knowing how to get along with employers; and knowing how to deal with sexual harassment and/or abuse.

6. "Marriage Enrichment for Young Couples"

Young married couples must make many adjustments, and so the church can become a resource to assist young couples in their formative years of marriage. Young married Black couples need help with issues such as the following: conflict and anger management; husband and wife roles; money management; praying, reading the Bible, and meditating together; dealing with in-laws; rearing children; and learning how to enrich and encourage each other.

7. "The Dangers of Drugs and Alcohol"

A large number of young Black adults have become the victims of illicit drugs, alcohol, and other addictive substances harmful to the body and mind. Regrettably, many of these young adults are married with mortgages, automobiles, and excessive debts, and thus the drug or alcohol habit becomes an additional burden on the individuals and their families. The church can become a haven of help for those who may become, or have become, addicted to illicit drugs.

Topics that may be explored include healthy self-esteem, human beings as made in the image of God, advice from a former substance abuser, what one needs to know about illicit drugs, and discussions led by a doctor and/or counselor.

8. "The Will of God for My Life"

Many young adults go through life without tapping into the great spiritual source of meaning found in Christ. The church can help singles and married couples explore their faith, engage in creative worship, study the Bible, know how to discern truth from error, and develop their spiritual gifts.

9. "Communicating with My Spouse"

My wife and I have been counselors and have served as workshop leaders for couples for more than 30 years. We have concluded that most couples could benefit immensely by learning how to communicate more effectively. Workshop and conference topic discussions could focus on these subjects:

- Knowing what to say after you say, "I do"
- Putting anger on hold
- Identifying and resolving conflict
- Making peace with one's spouse
- The relationship between bad conflict and good sex
- Reviewing marriage vows

10. "How to Cope with Depression"

Young African American adults must cope with many negative influences in their families, society, and personal lives. Many of these emotional, social, and interpersonal issues can be dealt with in a forthright and courageous manner through Christian education. Workshop and class topics can include defining depression, understanding the causes of depression, learning what the Bible has to say about depression, and discovering how to overcome depression.

By providing learning opportunities like these, the African American church can offer Mary, Tom, and other young adults the help they desperately need.

The following chart is intended to help the teacher enhance his or her awareness of young African American adults, their needs, concerns, and development.

OVERVIEW OF THE YOUNG ADULT YEARS: Ages 18–34

Life Events	Interpersonal Relationships
Entering vocational training or college	Teachers
First full-time employment	Career Models
Graduation from training or college	Peers of the same lifestyle
Leaving home; marriage and consummation	Sexual relationships
First child born	Spousal relationships In-law relationships Parent-child relationships
Relating anew to church and community	Pastoral relations Church membership
Establishing a career	Boss and work associates
Moving to a different area	Mentoring relationships
Children entering school	Marriage vs. singleness choice
Last child born	African American needs; adult concerns and development
Needs and Concerns	**Gifts**
Responsibility for one's affairs	Willingness to risk
Sense of vocational direction	Expanding knowledge
Close personal relationships with others	Creativity
Maturing relationship with one's parents	Intimacy
Growing abilities in daily work	Leadership roles
Maturing sense of one's role in history/society	Membership
Capacity to care for children	
Physical Development	**Intellectual Development**
Increased strength and coordination	Applies intellectual skill in intensive goal-directed study, work, and social participation
Body at peak performance	Commitment to lifelong learning
Increased acceptance of one's body	Mastering educational material Developing intellectual competence
Moral Development	**Spiritual Development**
Important for the community that all obey the laws—or work to change them	Loving God, self, and neighbor Learning to love, to care intimately for others
Moral chastity vs. unbridled passion	Bible study groups
Formation of ethical concepts	Affirmation of the beliefs, rituals, and symbols of the church as one's own
Establishing and choosing a Christian philosophy of life	Prayer; meditation; worship Acknowledgement of the traditions of other persons and cultures
Personal values	

CHAPTER 4

THE MIDDLE ADULT YEARS—THE BOOMER GENERATION

John and Nellie are in their midforties. John has worked for the post office for 25 years, and Mary is an elementary school teacher. They attend a church in their community and are active in the Sunday School and chancel choir. John is also a trustee of the church, while Nellie is a senior high Sunday School teacher.

John's father has Alzheimer's disease, and Nellie's mother and father are in a nursing home. John is concerned about his father and is deeply disturbed because he believes the nursing home has not been giving his father quality care. Furthermore, he has feelings of guilt because he, along with his sister, admitted his father to the nursing home. Neither he nor his sister was able to provide daily home care for their father, although John tried it for six months.

John and Nellie have three children. Ted, their older son, is in college. Their daughter, Martha, is a senior in high school. James, their younger son, dropped out of college two years ago and has been using illicit drugs. James has caused his parents to spend large sums of money due to skirmishes with the law and drug treatment in clinics. There is little evidence of James solving his problem. Both John and Nellie are at their wit's end about him. What can they do?

The pair has additional problems. For example, their daughter, Martha, will be graduating from high school in three months and wants to attend a university in another state. Unfortunately, they cannot afford the expense of out-of-state tuition and other connected expenses.

John and Nellie face many problems common to people in their age bracket. Feeling pulled in many directions and running out of resources, they can use every help the church can give.

CAUGHT IN THE MIDDLE

Nellie and John's stage in life is sometimes referred to as "middle age," but family and human development specialists do not fully agree on what to call it or how to define it. Carroll Kennedy defines middle adulthood as the ages between 35 and 50.[1] Some sociologists and adult educators, however, have broadened the age range of middle adults to reach to age 60. I lean toward this older age grouping in light of the Baby Boomer generation, many of whom have turned 60.

Middle adulthood is a time when many individuals are committed to achieving the goals they have planned. Adults in this stage of life tend to push harder to make up for wasted time in their earlier years. This second phase, middle adulthood, thus becomes a time of intense introspection with the reality of physical, psychological, and spiritual changes taking place in their lives. Some of the more obvious changes noted in middle adults are physiological changes, psychological/cognitive development, and spiritual and faith development.

PHYSIOLOGICAL CHANGES

Persons in middle adulthood see their bodies changing in a number of ways, mostly unwelcome. They may experience a decrease in hearing, seeing, and sexual prowess; men lose hair; and persons of both sexes see an increase in wrinkles and "middle-age spread" due to a decline in metabolism. There is also a decrease in testosterone and estrogen in men and women, respectively. With many Black males and females, late-onset diabetes and hypertension develop.

PSYCHOLOGICAL /COGNITIVE DEVELOPMENT

Middle adults have much on their minds. For many of them, this is a time of life when they worry over their careers, job satisfaction, and promotions. It can be a time of considerable stress for them as they reassess their dreams and aspirations and reevaluate their spiritual journeys. Sometimes going through the death or sickness of one or both parents, or caring for their aged parents, is a challenge. Middle adults may be concerned with giving time, talents, and gifts to a cause larger than themselves. They may also deal with the empty-nest syndrome, with children leaving home or going away to college.

SPIRITUAL AND FAITH DEVELOPMENT

Dr. James Fowler's book *Stages of Faith* describes the faith development that applies to many middle adults on their spiritual journeys. For the purpose of this book, I am including stages four and five of Fowler's discussions.

> *Stage Four.* The Individuative-Reflective Faith Stage begins when a person is willing to take responsibility for his or her own values, beliefs, and spiritual development. In this stage a person must raise the question, what is the meaning of my life? Or even more importantly, what do I truly believe? During this stage the adult seeks clear and concise answers for the unresolved faith questions that require definitive answers.
>
> *Stage Five.* Conjunctive Faith is the time when individuals begin to draw together a cohesive and comprehensive faith that one can acknowledge as one's own. It is what may be termed as "bought faith," and the adult is no longer threatened by the beliefs of others. In this stage faith is viewed as a unifying force that adds substance and structure to our lives. However, during this stage, the individual is still searching and seeking new truth and experiences to further clarify his faith.[2]

John Westerhoff describes a similar experience in his book *Will Our Children Have Faith?* In comparison with Fowler's stages four and five is what Westerhoff calls "owned faith."[3] Owned faith exists when we develop a personal belief with a strong degree of certitude. We have searched out our beliefs and have incorporated them into our lives. These beliefs have an inward confirmation and integrity, and we are willing to act upon them. This stage is a time of continued growth rather than a resting on past spiritual achievements. Prayer, Bible study, meditation, and witnessing of one's faith to others are some of the characteristics of this type of faith.

Havighurst's developmental theory of middle adulthood lists six developmental tasks. They are the following:

1. Achieving adult civic and social responsibility
2. Establishing and maintaining an economic standard of living
3. Assisting and [supporting] teenage children to become responsible and happy adults
4. Developing adult leisure time activities
5. Relating to one's spouse as an authentic person
6. Accepting and adjusting to the physiological changes that accompany the middle years[4]

TEACHING MIDDLE ADULTS

Let's take another look at John and Nellie. In ten years, John will be eligible to retire from the post office, having completed 35 years of service. He is concerned about what he is going to do with his spare time after retirement.

The church is an important part of the lives of John and Nellie. Most of their social life revolves around friends associated with their church. Both John and Nellie, however, have noticed that, except for a Sunday School class, there is little in their church's Christian education program for middle-aged adults.

How can the church help John and Nellie through this stage in their lives? Given the range of issues confronting their personal and family life, what kind of Christian education program can the local church create for middle-aged adults? Below are some suggested programs and classes for this age group:

1. "Enriching Your Marriage in the Middle Years"

A course or couples' retreat could allow couples to explore marital, sexual, social, and communicational strengths and weaknesses in their marriage relationship. Marriage enrichment retreats also offer couples the opportunity to meet other couples in an atmosphere of fellowship, fun, and relaxation. Often couples discover solutions through other couples who have experienced and solved problems similar to those they are facing.

2. "How to Deal with Troubled Adult Children"

A number of middle-aged adults have children with mental, social, academic, marital, and drug-related problems. Parents of these troubled young adults often put their own lives on hold while their young adult children persist in their plight. The church could create a support group to discuss the problems, and the stress and strain, created by adult children who contribute to family instability.

3. "Caring for an Aged and Sick Parent"

This class could be designed to help middle-aged adults deal with such topics as these: how to keep bonds of love with parents, how to take care of your parent's business affairs, what to do when your parent is in a nursing home, how to share responsibility for the parent with other family members, how to deal with anger, and how to handle your parent's estate.

4. "Planning for Retirement"

Middle adulthood is a time when individuals look forward to the retirement years. Many of them calculate current resources and project future contributions in order to establish a monetary figure for retirement. How much will they receive from pension, Social Security, and investments? Will they work after retirement? What plans will they make for leisure time? Will they have adequate health insurance benefits? Will they travel, and if so, how often? To what hobby or service activity will they give themselves? A church class could help middle adults answer these questions and realize that one's ability to serve is not limited by one's age but by one's willingness to be used by God.

5. "You Can Be a Mentor"

Middle-aged adults are a rich resource of experience and expertise. Usually they are still gainfully employed in a career or occupation where they have gained knowledge that can be shared with younger people. In my experience as a pastor, I have often been amazed at the number of people in the congregation who have professional and Christian experiences they could share to benefit younger members of the church. Pastors, ministers, Sunday School teachers, doctors, lawyers, nurses, administrators, skilled craftsmen, and other specialists, as well as laborers and homemakers, could mentor someone younger.

6. "Exploring My Christian Faith"

Many in this age group are in a quest to know more about God. They often are seeking a deeper walk of faith and desire to know more about the Bible. Some of the themes that can be studied in a class setting, therefore, include these: the meaning of faith; tests, trials, and temptation; the Bible and faith; teaching faith to my children; and physical healing and faith.

The middle adult years of the Boomers are prime time for learning, teaching, and mentoring.

The following chart is intended to help the teacher enhance his or her awareness of middle-age African American adults, their needs, concerns, and development.

OVERVIEW OF THE MIDDLE ADULT YEARS: Ages 35–60

Life Events	Interpersonal Relationships
Job Promotions	Neighbors
Church and community leadership	Friends
Marriage crisis; separation and/or divorce	Children's friends and their parents
First child leaves home	Work associates
First child marries	Spouse
Menopause	One's children as youth
25th wedding anniversary	Community agencies
First grandchild	Public figures
Career plateau	One's children as young adults
New career	Grandchildren
Death of parents	
Retirement	
Needs and Concerns	**Gifts**
Financial security for one's family	Dependability
Marital adjustments	Steadiness
Heavy demands of child rearing	Concern for the future
Creative, productive work in job or community	Financial resources
Self-esteem in the face of disappointments; Doubt	
Care and support for children in their new freedom	
Care of aged parents	
Exploration of new work and service options	
Physical Development	**Intellectual Development**
Tendency to add weight. Need for exercise	Through experience, gains greater perspective on personal, vocational, and social issues
Menopause and climacteric problems	Achieved academic preparation
Cardiac problems, especially for men	Professional careers
Problems with sight, hearing, teeth, surgery likely	
Moral Development	**Spiritual Development**
Decisions of conscience based on fulfillment of self-chosen ethical principles that are abstract, comprehensive, universal, consistent	Works creatively and productively to achieve God's will in all relationships; may fully integrate faith in life; may sense one's place in a universal community of faith

CHAPTER 5

THE OLDER ADULT YEARS—THE BUILDER GENERATION

The older adult years can be perceived by some as the years of decline. However, these years can also be a time of growth, excitement, and the exploration of newfound freedoms. Let us consider Patrick and Janice, both in their midsixties. Next year Patrick will turn 66 and will retire from his job of 35 years. Janice took an early retirement from her job as a secretary because of some health problems. They will both draw a pension, along with their security checks.

There is a problem, however, with Janice's health. She has been diagnosed with terminal cancer. Furthermore, the couple has a daughter who has recently gone through a divorce and has asked to move back home with them. In addition, the daughter has three teenaged children that will move in with her.

Patrick and Janice will need to make some important decisions about how they will handle Janice's health problems, Patrick's retirement, their daughter, and their three grandchildren.

If Patrick and Janice were members of your congregation, what are some of the Christian education programs your church could design to help them to cope with the issues confronting them?

Couples such as Patrick and Janice are considered to be older adults; that is, persons who are 60 years of age and older. Developmentally speaking, they are in the final stages of life and can expect, on average, to live another 20 to 25 years. Some of the developmental tasks of older adults can be summarized as follows:

1. Adjusting to decreasing physical strength and health

2. Retirement and less income to live on

3. Death or loss of one's spouse (usually husband)

4. Companionship and friendship with one's own age group

5. Assuming social, political, [religious], and civic responsibility

6. Seeking satisfactory living arrangements

7. Dealing with one's mortality

Slightly more than 1,000 Americans celebrate their 65th birthday daily. The number of older adults in the United States is approximately 30 million. Black Americans account for approximately 3 million, or 10 percent of the older adult population. It is estimated that the number of people 65 years and older will more than double by the middle of the twenty-first century to about 80 million.[1]

One of the great concerns that have far-reaching implications for African American churches is the number of Black women who will be left widowed as they become older. In 1994, for persons between 65 and 69 years of age, there were 982,000 African American males but 2.5 million females.[2] Certainly these numbers have serious implications for the kinds of programs and learning experiences churches ought to provide for the older adults in their congregations. For example, there is a need to help older persons to connect their faith with biblical truth; to face the reality of death and dying; to continue to grow in Christian maturity and God's grace; to manage one's resources as older families plan for the retirement years, while potentially dealing with limited income. Moreover, Christian education classes and other learning experiences should assist older adults in dealing with an emergent crisis and inevitable losses.

I have had the privilege of organizing fellowship groups designed specifically for older adults. These older adult groups meet weekly, bimonthly, or monthly, depending on how often they wish to meet. During their time together they share in activities that center on fellowship, evangelism, discipleship, Bible study, and Christian service. As the average age of the older population continues to increase, Black churches will need to develop creative programs addressing the needs of these adults. With improved health care, and better nutrition, we can expect further growth in this population. The American Association of Retired Persons has a membership of more than 20 million.

Ironically, merely growing older can become a complex problem in society, in churches, and in other dimensions of our lives. In his book *Old Age in a Changing Society*, Z. S. Blau makes a provocative statement.

> I do not deny the importance of the other problems that beset older people. Poverty, illness, inadequate and inappropriate housing are more widespread among the old than any other age group—but they are not unique to old age. I question the wisdom of a society that allocates considerable resources and talents to prolong human life, but fails to provide meaningful social [and spiritual] roles for older citizens. I submit it is the critical problem of aging in modern society.[3]

Why is it so important for the Black church to make use of its older members? Here are seven reasons.

1. **They have skills.** Older adults bring to the learning process a wealth of skills, knowledge, wisdom, and experiences acquired over many years. Much of what they know has become a treasure of experiences to be shared with those who are less initiated and less informed.

2. **They are motivated.** As people grow older, they come to realize that what they have learned over the years is worth sharing with others. The desire to help others is the driving passion that motivates a significant number of older people to leave their values, experiences, and contributions as personal legacies to posterity.

3. **They are discerning.** The years we have accumulated as older persons teach us how to evaluate and analyze knowledge, information, and circumstances in life. Older adults bring the gift of discernment to the learning environment. That gift becomes indispensable to the church as learners try to sort out truth from error and the essential from the trivial.

4. **They are reliable.** Older people tend to be dependable and can be counted on in our churches and society. Too often older adults are placed on the sidelines in our congregations, even though they are of sound mind and have valuable contributions to make to the church and the teaching ministry.

5. **They have influence.** We have all been influenced by older persons we have admired because of a piece of sage advice they have passed along to us. Lessons I learned from my grandparents are still deeply engraved in my mind.

Older adults may have tremendous influence on their families, friends, churches, and communities. They bring new and old contacts into their present and future.

6. **They are accessible.** Freed from the routine of a full-time job, many older adults enjoy being available to serve in the church. They also have more flexible schedules than do younger and middle adults, who have responsibilities of raising children and working full-time jobs.

7. **They are spiritually conscious.** Older people often have a compelling quest to know God more fully. And often it is time, and only time, that allows us to get in touch with those things that enhance and enrich our spiritual experiences. In the best case, as Christians become older adults, they also assume a mature posture of reverential strength and dignity.

FACTS ABOUT THE OLDER POPULATION AND THEIR IMPLICATIONS FOR BLACK CHURCHES

Christian educators would serve the African American church well by responding to the fact that our churches will have an extraordinary surge of senior adults over the coming years. The demand for ministries designed to meet the needs and address the concerns of this segment of the population is very real. Churches must be prepared to respond to the largest increase in our population to date. In a report titled, *65+ in the United States: 2005, Current, Population Reports, Special Studies,* U.S. Department of Human Services, 2005, the following facts and projections were noted:

1. In 1900 there were only 3.1 million elderly adults (60 years and above) in the United States. That number accounted for about 1 in 25 persons.

2. In 1990 there were 31.1 million elderly Americans. The number had grown 10 times greater than in 1900, with over 75 million adults born from 1946 to 1964. The Baby Boom contributed to one of the largest increases of the older adult population in the history of the United States. Life expectancy presently is about 75 years old.

3. By the middle of the twenty-first century, the elderly population could number over 79 million. However, the population of elderly between 67 and 74 is expected to peak at about 38 million in 2030.

4. The number of Black elderly is now approaching the 3 million mark and is expected to double in size by 2050. Of the 36.4 million African Americans, 8 percent of them are 60 and over.

5. America's most populous states are also those with the largest elderly populations. In fact, California, Florida, New York, Pennsylvania, Texas, Illinois, Ohio, Michigan, and New Jersey each has more than 1 million older adults. Many of them are African Americans living in urban centers including Chicago, New York City, Detroit, Cleveland, Houston, Philadelphia, Los Angeles, Miami, and Newark.

6. There were about 1.6 million older adults living in nursing homes in 1990. Of this 1.6 million, 1.3 million were females. The great majority, three in five were widowed. Elderly women outlive elderly men by an average of 10 years.[4]

In 1990 there were 18.6 million older women aged 65 and above. Meanwhile, older men in this age category numbered only 12.5 million. One conclusion we can draw from these statistics is that most elderly men have a spouse for assistance if their health fails, while the majority of elderly women do not. Still another conclusion to be drawn is that a substantial number of elderly women are living alone or in nursing homes.

A larger percentage of the Black elderly will likely be living in poverty than will their White counterparts. Consequently, as more of us live past 65 years, we face a greater chance of long-term illness, disability, lack of adequate income, and dependency on children and other family members. The overall economic picture for the elderly has improved since the mid-1970s, but there are still huge differences between the Black elderly and other minority groups.

IMPLICATIONS FOR MINISTRY TO THE BLACK ELDERLY

1. Based on what we already know about the elderly population in general, and the assumptions to be made about African American elderly, older people are some of the most valuable resources in our congregations.

2. Older adults have lived through various experiences in terms of family relations, trials, temptations, conflicts, sickness, death, and loneliness. Those

experiences can be passed on to younger generations in the form of teaching in Sunday School and the broader church activities.

3. Since the older adult population will continue to grow significantly, it is imperative that Black churches develop programs and educational experiences suitable to senior adults. There needs to be more homebound programs and activities, such as audio and video tape ministries and computer learning activities for older adults who are capable of operating them.

4. Churches must help older people have a better quality of life, and also help them prepare for dying. I have seen and known many Black elderly who were without a legal will at the time of their demise, leading to conflict among family members. There are many lessons to be drawn from the Old and New Testaments that could inspire the elderly to face death courageously.

5. The church, perhaps more than any other not-for-profit organization, uses volunteers in great numbers. The question is how to utilize the elderly members who are willing, able, and competent to work in the church. In some congregations, elderly persons work in nurseries, day care centers, the telephone ministry, and family centers, and they may serve as ushers, Sunday School teachers, counselors, and surrogate grandparents. The church must not retire or sideline persons when they reach the magic age of 65. A majority of adults 65 and older are mentally alert, emotionally stable, bodily strong, and ready to work. Rather than retire older persons, we need to allow them to make a transition to new places and positions of ministry in our congregations. As one older gentleman said to me: "Pastor, I am old but not cold." Older persons can be the burning embers to keep the church alive with a steady and consistent flame.

The two survey forms shown below may be used to help congregations discover the needs and kinds of resources they have among the older adults of their congregations. Often churches have hidden talent within this age group that is just waiting to be discovered.

SUGGESTED CHRISTIAN EDUCATION CLASSES, WORKSHOPS, AND CONFERENCES FOR OLDER ADULTS

Older adults have much to offer the rest of the church. They also have much they can still learn and experience in Christian education settings, even at this late stage of life. Ask the older adults in your church what they would like to talk about when they get together for Sunday School or other educational experiences. In the meantime, consider these suggested learning topics.

1. "Ministry with Older Adults"

Many older adults feel that their best years are behind them and do not see a bright future ahead. A class can be designed with them to rediscover some of the spiritual gifts and ministries they can continue through their church, in the community, and in senior citizen buildings where some live.

2. "Growing Old Gracefully and Godly"

Contrary to the prevailing thought in our society, not all seniors know how to grow old with dignity and grace. For many elderly people, growing old means the fear of losing instead of gaining in life. Many are experiencing a sense of loss that has affected how they view their physical strength, attractiveness, health, memory, spouses, children, self-esteem, and the control and competence they once had.

Psalm 71 is an excellent study about aging for use in a four-week study about growing old with grace and godliness. Here is an outline that can be used for a Bible study. (This outline can also become a 13-week Bible study for an older adult class.)

Topic: Growing Old Gracefully and Godly

Scripture: Psalm 71:1–24

Week One: God Is Our Refuge (v. 1)

God Is Our Rescuer (v. 2)

God Is Our Rock (v. 3)

God Is Our Helper (v. 4)

Week Two: Serving God from Generation to Generation (vs. 5–6)

A God Worthy of Praise (vs. 7–8)

Week Three: A God Who Will Not Forsake the Aged (vs. 9–13)

A God for Whom We May Witness (vs. 14–16)

A God Who Is Our Teacher (v. 17)

Week Four: A God of Power (v. 18)

A God Who Is Sovereign (v. 19)

A God of Restoration (vs. 20–21)

A God of Whom We Sing, Shout, and Praise (vs. 22–24)

3. "Looking Back over My Life"

When older adults take a backward glance, there is much for which they can feel appreciative. Many have lived full and enriched lives. The teacher or leader could ask each older adult to make a list of events or experiences they believe are worthy of sharing with others. The list they develop will be based on the following statements:

"WHEN I LOOK BACK OVER MY LIFE . . ."

Here are 10 things/experiences worth talking about.

1. My conversion:
2. An outstanding accomplishment or achievement:
3. A story about family members (grandchildren, mother/father, etc.):
4. My hobby:
5. A meal I like to make:
6. My favorite Bible verse, passage, or book of the Bible:
7. Places I have traveled:
8. A miracle in my life:
9. People who have made a difference in my life:
10. Three things for which I am thankful:

With some thought by and with these older adults, or Builders, a curriculum can be developed that will enhance their lives and the life of the church. The following three charts on pages 49–51 should assist those who are responsible for planning a program for older adults. These charts are intended to:

1. Help congregations identify volunteers and resource persons
2. Discover the felt needs of older adults to create more effective programs
3. Assist planners with an understanding of the different stages of growth and development that characterizes the lives of older adults

Senior Adult Ministry Opportunities

You are needed and of great value to God and to God's People.

NAME_____

ADDRESS_____

PHONE_____

FORMER OR PRESENT OCCUPATION_____

PLACES WHERE YOU WOULD SERVE IF NEEDED (Place a check mark next to all that apply.)

Outreach Ministry
❑ Missions Work
❑ Soul Winning
❑ Visit Prospects
❑ Outreach Leader
❑ Secretary
❑ Telephone Survey

Homebound Ministry
❑ Blind Ministry
❑ Deaf Ministry
❑ Mentally Impaired Children
❑ Tutoring Adults/Children
❑ Delivery Meals
❑ Visit Nursing Homes
❑ Home Bound Secretary
❑ Senior Transportation to Church
❑ Home Repair

Hospitality Ministry
❑ Healthcare Worker
❑ Cook Meals
❑ Serve Meals
❑ Hand Crafts
❑ Church Gardening

Community Ministry
❑ Red Cross Volunteer
❑ Clothes Closet Helper
❑ Adult Day Care
❑ Visitation
❑ Project Playpen

Church Ministry
❑ General Office Work
❑ Stuff Envelopes
❑ Arrange Flowers
❑ Projector/Video Operator
❑ Decorate for Socials
❑ Make Posters

Music Ministry
❑ Senior Choir Member
❑ Soloist
❑ Play Piano
❑ Choir Sponsor

Teaching Ministry
❑ Bible Study Leader
❑ Church History
❑ Work with Children
❑ Work with Youth

Please return this form to: _____

Older Adults Needs Assessment

The church needs your input to help determine the priority needs of older adults in our church and community. In the column of blanks beside the services listed, check 15 services you think are most needed among older adults. Return it by _____ [date] to _____ _____ [name and address]. Thank you for cooperating and helping with church planning.

[Pastor's name]

1. Friendly visitor program (companionship/run errands)	1. _____
2. Telephone reassurance services (daily or weekly calls)	2. _____
3. Handicapped transportation door-to-door	3. _____
4. Light housekeeping services (cook, dust, vacuum, mop, shop)	4. _____
5. Legal aid services	5. _____
6. Adult day care services	6. _____
7. Home health aide (give bath, shampoo, clip fingernails)	7. _____
8. Visually impaired rehabilitation services	8. _____
9. Day activities for active older adults	9. _____
10. Home emergency electronic response system	10. _____
11. Individual social assessment and service coordination	11. _____
12. Mental health counseling	12. _____
13. Hospice care (24-hour care for a short period)	13. _____
14 Van transportation (shopping, church, doctor, activities)	14. _____
15. Coordinate meal site	15. _____
16. Home-delivered meals	16. _____
17. Home chore services	17. _____
18. Information and referral services by telephone only	18. _____
19. On-site and telephone information and referral services	19. _____
20. Educational information on aging	20. _____
21. Home repair services (roof, heating equipment, plumbing)	21. _____
22. Advice and help processing insurance claims	22. _____
23. Guardianship/power of attorney	23. _____
24. Health counseling by a registered nurse	24. _____
25. Finding housing and relocation	25. _____
26. Counseling for transition to and from a health care facility	26. _____
27. Menu preparation assistance	27. _____
28. Legislative advocacy	28. _____
29. Are you 60+ years of age?	Yes_____ No_____

· ·(Detach Here)· ·

30. Volunteers are needed to help plan and develop an older adult program in this church. Please put your name and phone number below so we can talk about how you can help. Thank you for volunteering.

Name: _____ Phone: _____

Please return this form to: _____

OVERVIEW OF THE OLDER ADULT YEARS: Age 60 and Over

Life Events	Human Relationships
New leisure activities	Spouse and adult children
40th and 50th wedding anniversary	Church and organization friends
Transition into retirement	New group of older friends
Death of spouse; widowhood; remarriage	Grandchildren and great-grandchildren
Move to nursing home or to live with relatives	Mentor children, youth, and young adults
Needs and Concerns	**Gifts**
The desire to be needed	More time, wisdom, and objectivity
Major adjustment to retirement	More person-centered
Creative and useful investment of time	Triumph over suffering
Acceptance by persons and institutions	Acceptance of death as transition
Review and affirmation of one's life	Faith and hope
Human sharing in grief, joy, confusion	Biblical knowledge
Increasing health care	Share historical and family information
Limited mobility	
Close relationships decreasing through death	
Physical Development	**Intellectual Development**
Diminishing strength	Wisdom of many years' experiences
Need for exercise to retain physical activities	Intellectual power may decline, recall ability decreasing
Development of new skills	Loss in perception, reasoning memory
Chronic and terminal diseases	
Moral Development	**Spiritual Development**
Assumes wider circles of moral responsibility: family, church, school, community, nation, world	Strengthens and/or discovers integrity
	Affirming own life as having value, meaning, fulfillment
	Regards death (personal and others) with acceptance and hope
	Spiritual discernment

PART III:

TEACHING ADULTS
FOR LEARNING
AND LIVING

CHAPTER 6

THE SCOPE OF CURRICULUM IN AFRICAN AMERICAN CHURCHES

In the African American church, the challenge is to build a curriculum that will focus on the particular needs of Black people. The curriculum should be broad enough to include the many dimensions of the Black experience. To incorporate some of these concerns, the curriculum should do the following:

1. Incorporate African American images, history, and relevant experiences
2. Teach principles of liberation to free the minds of African Americans from the historical images of slavery, racism, prejudice, and discrimination
3. Equip the Black family and individuals with skills and resources to handle family, social, spiritual, personal, and interpersonal issues
4. Cover the life cycle and stages of Busters, Boomers, and Builders
5. Build dignity, self-esteem, and appreciation of our African heritage
6. Teach the Bible and church history from an Afro-centric point of view
7. Equip persons in urban environments to develop coping skills, refine values, and live creative, productive, victorious Christian lives
8. Prepare African American Christians to share the Gospel of Christ with the unsaved and unchurched

WHAT DO WE MEAN BY "ADULT"?

Some people define adulthood as the time when a person reaches a certain age. For others, adulthood comes about when the added weight of mature responsibility is laid upon one's shoulders. In our American culture, adulthood is often postponed until one completes high school. The privilege of driving an automobile and obtaining a driver's license is viewed as a rite of passage into young adulthood. There is truth associated with all of the above outlooks, but being an adult defies simplistic categories.

Contributing to the book, *Faith Development in the Adult Life Cycle*, Malcolm Knowles provides four broad definitions of the term *adult* that may be helpful. (1) The *biological* definition says one is an adult when one is able to reproduce babies. (2). The *legal* definition considers one an adult when one reaches the age at which the law states that a person can get a driver's license, buy liquor, enlist in the military, or marry without parental consent. (3) The *social* definition applies when a person starts performing the roles his or her culture assigns to the adult years. (4) The *psychological* definition considers someone an adult at the point where an individual perceives himself or herself as being basically responsible for his or her own life. The assumption to be drawn from these definitions is that adulthood is an ongoing process that encompasses all of the experiences that impact one's maturation and development in the post adolescent period of life.[1]

Adulthood is more than reaching a chronological age that society and our laws have decreed. Perhaps it is more accurate to say that adults are persons who have assumed an attitude that motivates them to accept and perform adult responsibility and give up childish ways. An adult is one who has cut the umbilical cord from mother and father in order to grow and develop into a mature person. It does not mean one no longer continues a loving and healthy relationship with mother and father. Being an adult is not alienation from family and friends; rather it is a reordering and reevaluation of the way one perceives adult maturity. Paul's words to the Corinthians is a fitting summary here: "When I was a child, I talked like a child, I thought like a child, I reasoned like a child. When I became a man [an adult], I put childish ways behind me" (1 Corinthians 13:11, NIV).

CURRICULUM PLANNING ASSUMPTIONS

Here are some key assumptions to be considered when planning for the African American Christian adult learners, based on the essential differences between children and adults.

1. Christian adult learners perceive God as the ultimate source of knowledge, wisdom, and truth.

2. Christian adult learners are admonished throughout the Bible to grow in grace and knowledge (2 Peter 3:18), to grow into perfection (Ephesians 4:16), to grow into mature persons, and to grow to the fullness of the stature of Christ (Ephesians 4:13).

3. Christian adult learners view learning as an opportunity *and* a God-given right.

4. Christian adult learners are motivated to learn as they experience needs and interests that learning will satisfy. These are appropriate learning points for organizing adult learning activities.

5. Christian adult learning is life centered. Therefore, the appropriate units for organizing adult learning are life situations, not prescribed subjects.

6. Christian adult learners' richest resources are their experiences; therefore, the core methodology of adult education is the analysis of experience. Christian adult learners have a deep need to be self-directing; hence, the role of the teacher is to engage learners in a process of mutual inquiry rather than a transmission of knowledge or an insistence on conformity.

7. With increase in age, individual differences as expressed in lifestyles and needs are magnified. Therefore, adult education must make optimal provisions for differences in style, time, place, and pace of learning.

The African American church that keeps these distinct assumptions between children and adults will increase the attendance and effectiveness of its adult learning experiences.

A HOLISTIC APPROACH TO CURRICULUM DEVELOPMENT

Christian education takes on a relevant meaning when it orders the way we live, reflects how we respond to God, and shapes how we behave toward each other. The effective curriculum, therefore, is based on where people live, work, and play. It touches every facet of the adult's spiritual, social, and psychological being. It helps people to love God and value the Golden Rule—doing good to others as we want others to do good to us.

In this section, I am proposing what I call a "total curriculum." This curriculum is not centered in secular and humanistic philosophy—but in Jesus Christ. It is not steeped in heavy, incomprehensible theological jargon that makes little or no sense to the average layperson in our African American churches, but rather it provides the rule and reason behind our educational ministry and mission. In "Trends in Christian Education," B. T. Roberts makes this powerful statement: "If we are really following Christ, we shall observe his precepts where they come in conflict with the customs of the day. No one can be a follower of the fashions, and a follower of Christ. If we go with Christ only so far as the proud and the world go, and leave him where they leave him, then it is the world we are following, not Christ."[2] Through the comprehensive Christian education practices of a total curriculum, we must continue to lift up Christ, for He promised if we will do our part, Jesus Himself would draw all men (see John 12:32).

CURRICULUM GOALS

There are four goals of a total curriculum.

1. Enabling Christians to Share Their Love

Our teaching ought to motivate learners to love as Jesus loved. Effective Christian education encourages people to know and understand what it means to love their neighbor and have a love relationship with Christ. Love is more than abstract language void of action; it is a living relationship. Love is the reflection of God's goodness, righteousness, and truth in daily life. The lessons taught from the written pages must become the incarnate Word lived out in loving relationships among the people of God. There are numerous verses in the Bible that challenge us to love God and each other. A brief explanation from the Old and New Testaments reveals the following truths about love: "Love the LORD your God with all your heart and with all your soul and with all your strength" (Deuteronomy 6:5); "Love the LORD, all his saints! The LORD preserves the faithful, but the proud he pays back in full" (Psalm 31:23); "And I pray that you, being rooted and established in love, may have power, together with all the saints" (Ephesians 3:17). Many other Scriptures emphasize the importance of loving one another, including John 16:27 and 17:26, Galatians 5:22, and 1 Peter 1:8.

2. Equipping the Laity

In addition to teaching people to love, a total curriculum should also equip people to labor in God's vineyard. Our "vineyard" is wherever people live and interact with one another. The call of Christ to all disciples is to work while it is day, for when night comes no one will be able to work (John 9:4). It is imperative, therefore, for the church to instill the principles of the "work of ministry" and to expand the kingdom of Christ in the lives of people.

Teaching that is centered in Christ is essentially an equipping ministry. In this quality of ministry, the pastor and the teaching staff view their assignment as helping those in the church to (a) discover the nature and function of their ministry, and (b) educate, equip, and empower people to share their faith. Christians are called to be ministers and not just church members. In many of our African American churches, a critical issue is the inadequate and insufficient number of persons who are prepared to do ministry beyond the walls of their congregations.

Even more challenging are those who have never viewed themselves as ministers of the Gospel. Many have not been taught how to share their faith with others. Thus a fundamental part of equipping for ministry is teaching adults how to be good students of the Bible. It is not to be assumed that persons are biblically literate due to their longevity in the church. Neither can we infer that persons have knowledge of the Bible based on their church attendance. Nothing short of rigorous and systematic investigation of Scripture will develop a well-equipped adult learner. The degree to which adults function as witnesses for Christ in the world is directly related to how well the church has equipped them in the Word and work of the church.

3. Praying

Harold Carter believes that the Black prayer tradition must be seriously rethought and consciously revived if this valuable resource of traditional spiritual power is to serve the needs of Black persons in today's world.[3] Jesus taught His disciples to pray on numerous occasions (Matthew 18:19–20; Mark 1:35; Luke 11:1–4; 18:1–6). And so we must conclude that a church that emphasizes teaching and sound doctrinal principles to the exclusion of prayer will not succeed in fulfilling its mandate from Christ.

Praying churches are powerful churches. As Christians, we must never forget that we can learn more in an hour before God than we can in hours of preparation without Him. It is our quiet devotional times with Christ that give us the insights and spiritual resources we need to conquer in the warfare with demonic forces. E. M. Bounds, a prolific writer on prayer, once said, "What the Church needs today is not more machinery, or better organizations or more and novel methods, but men [and women] whom the Holy Ghost can use. Men [and women] of prayer—who are mighty in prayer. The Holy Ghost does not flow through methods, but through people. He does not come on machinery, but on people."[4]

Through prayer, God gives plans and His Holy Ghost fills people. May God grant the church vision and determination to prepare people to become diligent prayer warriors and students.

4. Building Community

Unity, solidarity, and Christian relationships are the principles for which the church strives. The church in the book of Acts was a church where true community was evidenced. "They devoted themselves to the apostles' teaching and to the fellowship, to the breaking of bread and to prayer" (Acts 2:42, NIV). The Greek word for "fellowship" is properly rendered *koinonia* and can be used in several ways.[5] It can be interpreted to mean participation, or purposive partnership. At a more profound level, though, this term carries two other related meanings: (1) to share and participate together in a common partnership; and (2) to share our material blessings by giving to others.

In order for a church to be Christo-centric, it must teach members how to live in community with one another. Paul admonished the Christians at Rome and Ephesus to live in Christian fellowship as brothers and sisters:

> Just as each of us has one body with many members, and these members do not have the same function, so in Christ we who are many form one body, and each member belongs to all the others (Romans 12:4–5, NIV).
>
> From Him [Christ] the whole body, joined and held together by every supporting ligament, grows and builds itself up in love, as each part does its work (Ephesians 4:16, NIV).

In other words, the main feature of a Christian community is that it functions as a unit, and through its functioning, the entire body of Christ gains individual and corporate integrity.

When congregations seek to teach and equip adults to build strong Christian relationships, the following will be true: (1) They will realize the strength, vigor, and close fellowship of believers who know how to reach out to others, because they first learned how to reach inward to themselves. (2) They will realize a community of believers who place strong emphasis on worship through praise and exuberant celebration. (3) The focus of this kind of church will be centered on the people as a whole and not exclusively on the pastor.

COMMUNITY IN CHRIST

When it comes to the fourth goal, there is one other point we must recognize: we can never have real community with each other without first experiencing community with Christ. Teaching our members to cultivate an authentic relationship with Christ is foundational for every other relationship inside as well as outside the body of Christ. Consequently, the Christian community is not based on kinship, friendship, cliques, clubs, or fraternities. The community of God is based on redemption from sin and unity through His Holy Spirit. Therefore, it is bigger and better than any other human group.

When the church finds community in Christ, she is at her best. We can affirm the words of Andrew W. Byers, who wrote these lines regarding the oneness of community found in the church:

The Church Has One Foundation

The Church has one foundation,
    Tis Jesus Christ her Lord.
She is the new creation,
    Through water by the Word.
From heav'n, He came and sought her,
    To be His holy Bride;
With His own blood He bought her,
    And for her life, He died.

Elect from every nation,
    Yet one o'er all the earth.

> Her charter of salvation—
>> One Lord, One faith—One birth.
>
> One holy name she blesses,
>> Partakes one holy food,
>
> And to one hope she presses
>> With every grace endued.
>
> Back to the one foundation,
>> From sects and creeds made free,
>
> Come saints of every nation
>> To blessed unity.
>
> Once more the ancient glory
>> Shines as in days of old,
>
> And tells the wondrous story—
>> One God, One faith, One fold.[6]

Along the same lines, in his book, *True Fellowship*, Jerry Bridges wrote,

> All believers share a common life in Christ, whether or not we recognize it. We are in fellowship with literally thousands of believers from every nation of the world. . . . This objective truth of Koinonia is meant to provide the foundation for the experiential aspects of fellowship. The realization that we do in fact share a common life with other believers should stimulate within us a desire to share experientially with one another. . . . This is the whole thrust of the New Testament teaching on Koinonia.[7]

The curriculum goal of community, then, produces wonderful relationships, first with Christ, and then through Him, with our fellow Christians.

To summarize, a holistic approach to curriculum development includes (1) enabling Christians to share their love, (2) equipping the laity for ministry, (3) encouraging the church to pray, and (4) building a community of unity and fellowship. These goals help meet the broad-based needs of adults of all generations.

CHAPTER 7

DISCOVERING SPIRITUAL GIFTS

In my travel and service to congregations around the nation and in foreign countries, I have witnessed wasted talent among many congregations, though not because people in the pew lack the desire to be used by God. Hundreds of individuals have wondered, and have even asked, how do I get a chance to share my ministry in the church, the community, and the world?

A total curriculum church graciously opens its arms and hearts to the leading of the Holy Spirit to prepare men and women to engage their spiritual gifts. The essential issue of ministry is not to be decided based on academic degrees nor family pedigrees but on the humility and availability with which Christians present themselves to God for service. Pastors and church leaders will do well to bring new life and energy into their congregations by incorporating the gifts ordained by God for His church. I believe the unleashing of laypersons to do ministry will free pastors and overworked and overstressed church leaders to be more effective in the service of our Lord.

Indeed, no church can effectively operate without helping its members discover, cultivate, and exercise their spiritual gifts. Deploying spiritual gifts in a congregation is both biblically correct and absolutely necessary. Without the operation and utilization of spiritual gifts, congregations cease to live up to their full potential for ministry within and outside the walls of their churches. Thus teaching people to discover and use spiritual gifts should be an integral part of education in African American congregations.

WHAT ARE
SPIRITUAL GIFTS?

The issue of spiritual gifts is new or murky to some in our churches, and therefore we must spend some time reviewing what these gifts are, why they exist, and how we should go about using them.

Simply put, spiritual gifts are special abilities given to Christian believers by the Holy Spirit. He equips, qualifies, and commissions believers to serve the church and the world through dynamic spiritual ministries. When spiritual gifts are rightfully recognized and employed in our churches, they will enable the local congregation to mobilize their members to share in ministry, develop spiritual leaders, and foster a spirit of cooperation and interdependence.

The Lord has equipped the church to exercise its spiritual gifts by applying wisdom (see 1 Corinthians 12). Each of the gifts mentioned in this passage is manifested through administration, teaching, counseling, preaching, evangelism, caring, and preaching (see 1 Corinthians 12:4–11, 28).

The Bible teaches us that spiritual gifts are given for three purposes:

1. That Christians may minister to each other in the body of Christ. Gifts are given "for the common good" (1 Corinthians 12:7, RSV). We ought to "employ our gifts for one another" (1 Peter 4:10).
2. That the body of Christ may be built up, that is, grow in unity and maturity in Christ (Ephesians 4:11–16). As believers use their gifts, the church's witness and ministry are extended in the world (Acts 1:8).
3. That God may be glorified. Peter observed that God will be glorified in everything if believers, exercising their spiritual gifts, speak the Word of God in the strength God supplies (1 Peter 4:11).[1]

To fully understand the priesthood of all believers and how spiritual gifts operate in the church, effective Black congregations are abandoning the practice of service by seniority and ministry based on favoritism. For too long, pastors and church leaders have operated on the premise of selecting persons who agree with them and share their philosophy of ministry. Congregations need to be rescued from the grip of marginal ministry by liberating members to share their spiritual gifts.

The gifts of the church can best reach their full potential when they are called forth by the Holy Spirit's election, not merely by human selection.

A FRESH INTEREST IN SPIRITUAL GIFTS

In his excellent book titled *Glory to the Spirit,* the late Bishop Benjamin F. Reid offers this advice to churches: "The Holy Spirit is making the church more aware of the need for the practice of spiritual gifts. Despite some abuses of spiritual gifts, the church has become keenly aware of the fact that it cannot adequately or properly operate without the impartation of the gifts of the Spirit."[2] Bishop Reid continues by saying that "no longer are spiritual gifts seen as priceless possessions of a favored few but as God's universal provision for the entire Church, enabling ordinary men and women to achieve extraordinary results for God."[3]

Why is there such a renewed interest in spiritual gifts? I think there are several factors:

1. A new concern for the ministry of all believers. In the last few decades, there has been a serious concern about using laypersons in the various ministries of the church. To be sure, clergy have tended to dominate and control ministerial service. However, there has been an increasing interest on the part of laypeople to examine their roles in the light of scriptural authority.

2. The search for intimate, less institutionalized church structures. Both pastoral and lay leadership have grown disillusioned and discontent with inflexible church structures and desire to make the leadership of the church more inclusive. In their quest for more inclusive opportunities to function in ministry, pastors and leaders have taken a new look at the concept that every believer is a minister. It is virtually impossible to study the New Testament church without sensing the strong emphasis on spiritual gifts in the life of the church.

3. A renewed interest in the study of the Bible. Part of the renewed interest in spiritual gifts has grown out of a new concern to accept the Bible as a book that encourages the discovery and development of spiritual gifts. The church, since its inception, has been charismatic (gifted by the Holy Spirit). With this fresh anointing, it stands to reason that this important truth should resurface as a dominant Bible teaching in the twenty-first century.

The verse of a song that we sing in my church brings home the truth of this biblical mandate for the development of spiritual gifts:

> God sets her members each in place
> According to His will.
> Apostles, prophets, teachers, all—
> His purpose to fulfill.[4]

The development and cultivation of spiritual gifts in our congregations is not an option; it is a requirement. Therefore, it is the task of the leadership of every congregation to prepare its members to make full use of their spiritual gifts.

The following process, if fully employed by the leadership, will help its members to comprehend a basic understanding of their spiritual gift(s);

- prayerfully seek the Holy Spirit to identify the spiritual gift(s) they have been given;
- consecrate themselves for spiritual service;
- confirm their spiritual gifts through the discernment of other Christians who are spiritually minded;
- continue to ask the Holy Spirit to help them to refine their spiritual gift(s).

PART IV:

CHRISTIAN EDUCATION AND THE FAMILY

CHAPTER 8

FAMILY LIFE EDUCATION IN THE CHURCH

An old adage says, "As the family goes, so goes the church." Few, if any, would deny the importance of building strong families in our congregations. Yet many are unable to make the connection between strong families and strong churches. Aren't the two integrally linked? When our families are strong and healthy, our churches will likewise be strong and healthy.

The relationship between the church and the family is highlighted in the statements that follow:

1. The church and the family are united in spiritual and interpersonal relationships that require commitments toward growth in understanding, love, and spiritual renewal.

2. The church and the family are highly related in helping to build solid social, political, educational, and religious foundations in the community.

3. The church and the family are involved in societal and institutional changes and are challenged to discover solutions to avoid dysfunction and moral decline.

4. The church can help parents and children work toward bridging the generation gap of opposing philosophies, practices, and values.

5. The church is challenged to help families deal with family conflict, role confusion, and the formation of viable family relationships.

6. The church is challenged to see how its resources can help families address and solve family relationships.

7. The Black church is challenged to find ways to develop family related

programs, activities, and resources to assist families in their efforts to grow in mature relationships.

BASIC ASSUMPTIONS

These are my five basic assumptions about family life education in a church setting:

1. The biblical mission of the church is to minister to families in creative and dynamic ways.
2. The church is in a unique position to minister to families.
3. The church is called to minister by addressing the spiritual, social, emotional, and educational needs of its members.
4. Many churches possess a variety of people, resources, and social networks that can help meet the needs of its members, its community, and those beyond its local boundaries.
5. In times of family crises, the church and the pastor may bring healing and hope to broken and bewildered families.

BIBLICAL GUIDELINES
FOR THE BLACK FAMILY

The Bible is an important resource in planning Christian education for African American families. Principles found in Scripture help to create healthy family relationships and educational programs to enrich family life. The history of salvation begins with a single family—Adam and Eve—and climaxes with the church as the metaphor of the family of God. Both Old and New Testaments illustrate concepts about the family that deserve the church's thoughtful attention.

Salvation and the Black family. The biblical idea of the family is more extended than nuclear. Writers in both Old and New Testaments are careful in mentioning families, clans, tribes, and nations. Major genealogies are recorded in Genesis 10, 1 Chronicles 1, Matthew 1:1–16, and Luke 3:23–28.

These Bible passages are extremely valuable because they trace the salvation history of Black people. Although there have been attempts by a number of White Bible scholars, historians, and anthropologists to dismiss the Black presence in the

Bible, the evidence for that presence is overwhelming. For instance, we are told that from the lineage of Ham (whose name can be translated "hot, sunburned, or black") came the following nation-families: the Canaanites, the Egyptians (Mizraim), the Philistines, the Hittites, and the Amorites.

A well-known Southern White Bible scholar, J. Vernon McGee (now deceased), made this provocative comment concerning Black people in the Bible:

> The first great civilizations came out from the sons of Ham. We need to recognize that. It is so easy today to fall into the old patterns that we were taught in school a few years ago. Now the black man is wanting to study more of his race. I don't blame him. He hasn't been given an opportunity in the past several hundred years. The story of the black man is that he headed up the first two great civilizations that appeared on earth. They were the sons of Ham. Nimrod was a son of Ham [and a mighty warrior and builder of cities (Genesis 10:9–12)].[31]

Through the genealogical records, the Bible has provided documentation from Adam to Christ. In Matthew's gospel, the lineage of Christ is traced to Joseph, Christ's earthly father. In Luke, Jesus is traced to Mary, His earthly mother. However, His true genealogy is traced back to God (Luke 3:38).

When family life education is taught and presented within the context of biblical salvation, it takes on a new position in the teaching ministry of the church. Black people are able to locate their identity, which reaches back thousands of years in biblical history.

The Marriage Relationship. The Bible speaks of how man and woman are to relate to one another. More specifically, in Genesis 2:24 and Ephesians 5:31 we find the three steps that take place in marriage: (1) A man leaves his father and mother. (2) He is united with his wife. (3) The two become one flesh in sexual union.

We learn from these verses of Scripture the true meaning of marriage. Marriage is first leaving (note: not forsaking) one's mother and father. It is coming of age and growing into maturity, a time when a man and a woman cut the parental umbilical cord and begin to grow into adulthood. Other parts of the marriage may be negotiated, but not the leaving. Leaving is a sign that the couple has accepted the role of responsible decision-making and no longer relies on their parents to order their thoughts and decisions.

The second principle we learn from this verse is taken from an archaic word used in the King James Version: "cleaving." It means to be joined or solidly connected together. Perhaps it is safe to say that when we are married, we are glued together. I am not projecting the idea that married people are stuck with each other. This "glue" to which I refer is sacred and sanctified, and it binds the marriage partners together through bonds of committed love.

"Cleaving" to each other means building a strong and solid marital relationship. Couples cleave when the fierce winds of destruction blow; they cleave when the fiery flames of discomfort seem unbearable; they cleave in sickness and health; they cleave in times of plenty and want, for better and for worse. Accepting our differences and growing despite our conflicts—this is what cleaving is all about. Cleaving can produce a closeness that strengthens the marriage commitment, until nothing is more important to the couple than their togetherness.

The third principle is "becoming one flesh," or coming together in unity. It is the "becoming" aspect of this principle that I want to emphasize here.

What distinguishes love from lust is loyalty. Married couples are challenged to learn early in their marital relationship that the sexual act is the result of who you are when you are in relationship with the person you love. This type of love is more than a duty or obligation. We become one flesh because we have grown to care, share, and bear each other's burdens and joys. In a sense, a Christian marriage represents what couples have suffered, endured, overcome, and experienced together.

In Ephesians 5:25 and 28, we find two commands that Paul gave to husbands: (1) a man is to love his wife as Christ loved the church; and (2) he is to love his wife as his own body, by nourishing and cherishing her. The Greek word *eletreho* (nourish) puts forth the idea of helping someone to grow to his or her full potential psychologically, socially, spiritually, and emotionally. In a similar manner, the word "cherish" is from a Greek word *thalpo*, and it means to keep warm. The love that a husband and wife have for each other facilitates a warm and growing love relationship. The love that Christ has for the church is sacrificial, self-giving love that brings about a bond of fellowship and unity for a married couple.

Instructions to Parents. Children have always needed guidance and instruction, and in the Bible, parents are charged with instructing and leading their children. Although parental authority in Bible times far exceeded such authority today, many children back then were still unruly, unthankful, and undisciplined. Consider the following verses:

> They shall say unto the elders of the city, This our son is stubborn and rebellious, he will not obey our voice; he is a glutton, and a drunkard (Deuteronomy 21:20, KJV).
>
> A wise son maketh a glad father: but a foolish man despiseth his mother (Proverbs 15:20, KJV).
>
> There is a generation that curseth their father, and doth not bless their mother (Proverbs 30:11, KJV).
>
> Men shall be lovers of their own selves, covetous, boasters, proud, blasphemers, disobedient to parents, unthankful, unholy (2 Timothy 3:2, KJV).

Despite the challenges that parents have always faced in raising their children, the Bible does not let them off the hook for doing their best for their children. Here are six specific commands from the Bible to parents:

1. Parents are to teach their children (Deuteronomy 6:7).
2. Parents are to train a child in the right way (Proverbs 22:6).
3. Parents are to provide for their children (2 Corinthians 12:14).
4. Parents are to discipline in the counsel of the Lord (Ephesians 6:4).
5. Deacons are to manage their children and household well (1 Timothy 3:12).
6. Younger women are to love their husbands and their children (Titus 2:4).

Given the rationales in my basic assumptions and biblical guidelines for family life, African American congregations are challenged to find ways to minister to Black families under their care. Can the Black church live up to this challenge? In the next chapter we will consider why and how the African American church can help the family fulfill biblical mandates.

CHAPTER 9

HOW TO PLAN MINISTRIES WITH FAMILIES

Why should African American churches build programs to strengthen the Black family? Consider these five stimulating reasons:

1. The Black family has shown marvelous survival skills through extraordinary hardship.
2. The concept of the extended family has greatly aided the Black family in overcoming the vestiges of slavery, segregation, and institutional racism.
3. Ideals and values cherished by Black people address family roles and structures and have contributed to the strength and dignity of the Black family.
4. The church has the responsibility to assist families in shaping roles, interpersonal relationships, and values.
5. The church is in the business of planning programs, activities, and ministries that will strengthen family life throughout the life cycle.

An effective ministry with families grows out of a strong mix of sensitivities to people, good planning, care, timing, and clear thinking—all under the influence of God's Spirit. What follows is an outline of some of the ways pastors, planners, directors of family life, and others can acquire tools to plan and promote family life programs for the church.

CONSIDERING THE RATIONALE

Certain undeniable truths underscore for us the importance of the church supporting the family—through education and by many other means.

The home forms the basic support for the church. The New Testament indicates that early churches often met in homes (Acts 2:46; Romans 16:3–5; Colossians 4:15). It can be assumed, then, that the church and the home are to be allies in impacting the family unit. As one complements the other, the church's mission of teaching biblical revelation will become easier and more effective.

Down through the centuries, Christian churches have recognized the importance of the family as the basic social unit to perform certain essential functions in society and the kingdom of God. Among these functions are nurturing children, teaching family values, strengthening marriages, and helping individuals and families cope with life issues.

The church helps families throughout the family life cycle. It gives attention to the developmental concerns at each stage of the family life cycle. In doing so, the church plans for families as well as for individuals.

The church gives to its families the kind of help that enables them to provide Christian nurture within the family. The church encourages family members to mature in the Christian faith, learn good communication skills, and rear children with Christian love and discipline.

Finally, the church carries the responsibility for helping families to be the church in the world. There are many opportunities for families to serve and witness to individuals and families within their immediate community.

DEFINING YOUR PURPOSE

A worthwhile enterprise must clearly define its purpose for being. What is the purpose of family life education and ministry in the church? A broad purpose of family ministry for local congregations is to minister to individuals and families in various stages of their development. This includes married couples, singles, older adults, children, and youth.

Few will disagree with that statement of purpose. But some may ask, "Where do we go from here?" Good question. And my response is that one of the initial concerns for family life programming should be determining the felt needs of congregational families.

Here are some fundamental questions to ask when doing a needs assessment:

1. What do individuals need in order to function as helpful family members?
2. What do family units—all kinds of families—need to function most effectively?
3. What forces are affecting families in your church and community? Which of these are destructive and should be opposed or overcome? Which are positive and should be reinforced?
4. What are some of the potentialities for your families' growth and ministry?
5. Which of these possibilities should be stimulated or strengthened?

Here are two survey forms that can help determine some of the needs of families in your church.

FAMILY ASSESSMENT SURVEY FORM

This form is designed for local boards of Christian education or Christian education committees to evaluate the quality and types of family life education offered to its members. The survey should be completed by a minimum of 20 to 25 members who are knowledgeable of the congregations.

Once the survey has been completed, the results should be tabulated and shared with the congregation. Programs should then be planned which address some of the needs discovered in the survey.

Family Survey Form

General Concern	None	Little	Some	Much
Premarital education	___	___	___	___
Couple enrichment	___	___	___	___
Family worship	___	___	___	___
Living the single life	___	___	___	___
Family financial planning	___	___	___	___
Teaching Christian values	___	___	___	___
Sex education for teens	___	___	___	___
Parent education	___	___	___	___
Intergenerational meetings	___	___	___	___
Growing old gracefully	___	___	___	___
Planning for retirement	___	___	___	___
Family Bible study	___	___	___	___
Parent-child communication	___	___	___	___
Coping with death	___	___	___	___

Family Needs Survey

Families move through different developmental stages. This work sheet will help identify the needs of each phase of family life. (Make additions or adaptations for other groups.) The priority rating should be based on a 1, 2, 3 rating scale, with 1 being less important, 2 being important, and 3 being very important.

Developmental Phase	Needs	% in Congregation	Strategy to Meet Needs	Priority Rating
Beginning Families				
Families with elementary school children				
Families with teenagers				
Families in the launching stage				
Families in the middle years				
Aged families				

A STRATEGY FOR MINISTRY

To get started in the right direction for your family ministry, you will need to organize persons who carry a burden for families and who have some abilities and skills to get the job done. This group could become the nucleus of a family ministry task force or committee. Their enthusiasm will be invaluable, but it is also important to remember that a church should move slowly and plan carefully so that a family ministry program does not end in confusion and frustration.

In addition to organizing your family life committee, here are a few suggestions for getting started in the church:

1. **Develop family awareness and appreciation.** Guide church leadership to evaluate what is already being done in terms of family ministry and what should be started.

2. **Do a personal study on family life.** Whether you are a clergy member or a layperson, you will be able to speak and share from a stronger position of understanding if your reading on family life is current.

3. **Guide church leadership in study.** Ask that church leaders take turns reading a book on marriage and family life and then presenting a brief review at a board meeting.

4. **Have resources available for the congregation.** Be sure your church library has an ample section of books, tapes, magazines, and other resources on marriage and family life.

5. **Develop a family ministry task force.** Such a task force may include current church leaders, but it could also involve several people from the congregation who have a concern for families and their development. Be sure to invite someone to be a part of this task force who will represent children and youth.

6. **Plan informal intergenerational activities.** Offer special events such as intergenerational workshops or fellowship experiences. Summer is often a time when other activities have shut down for several weeks, so this can be an excellent time to offer something new and exciting.

7. **Evaluate results.** Seldom, if ever, is a program without need for improvement, especially the first time around. So utilize staff meetings, comments of participants, and more formal feedback from questionnaires for program

revision. In addition, here are some questions to consider when analyzing the information collected on the survey sheets:

- What kinds of people and resources are in the congregation to assist in meeting discovered needs?
- What community agencies are there from which experts may be recruited for family workshops?
- How can our church help families address identified issues?
- What are the resources and services to which some families may be referred?
- Can you list some of the ways the church can empower a family to fulfill its biblical mandate? How may biblical patterns of behavior help family members fulfill God's intent for the family?
- What kind of criteria will be established for assigning a priority rating to family needs? (Suggestion: Family needs could be rated on a scale from 1 through 3, with 1 receiving the highest priority.)

The church in every generation is challenged to counteract the unbridled destruction designed to destroy family spirituality and values. The Black family is being attacked daily by the drug pushers, agents who distribute alcohol in our communities, and the influence of pornography, crime, and immorality. Thus it is imperative that we set a strategy to minister to the entire family.

This chapter has placed a strong emphasis on the planning process that brings about more effective ministry to adults as leaders of the family. The writer strongly believes that the church should be at the forefront in assisting adults to become better parents, strengthening couples by enriching their marriages, and building their self-esteem throughout their life cycles.

CHAPTER 10

BIBLE STUDIES
FOR THE FAMILY

The following four sessions have been designed to help families become better acquainted with the Bible. Each of the sessions involves a Bible study along with some exercises to involve all participants in the group. These sessions are suitable for married couples, adult Sunday School classes, or any other group interested in learning more about marriage and family living from a biblical perspective.

An essential part of the planning process to meet family needs is to develop a methodology to help the church plan programs that will reach families at various stages of the life cycle. As one complements the other, the church's mission of teaching the biblical revelation will become easier and more effective.

The intention of the following Bible studies is to explore what the Bible teaches about marriage and family relationships. Adults Bible study produces a wealth of information when the inductive study method is utilized. Inductive Bible studies are constructive and beneficial because adults gain an understanding of the Bible by responding to the biblical text with relevant questions. For example:

- What is the author saying?
- To whom is the author speaking?
- What was the meaning of the words in the text when the author wrote them?
- How does the text apply to my life today?

Moreover, a church whose emphasis is on teaching biblical principles will inspire persons to appreciate and study the Bible for personal enrichment and spiritual development.

EXPLORING MARITAL AND FAMILY RELATIONSHIPS

Session 1: "God's Purpose in Marriage"

Time: 1 1⁄2 hours

Materials needed: Chalk, chalkboard, flip chart, pencils, scratch paper

Reflection: Becoming one flesh means much more than just achieving physical union. It means that two persons share everything they have—not only their bodies, not only their material possessions, but also their thinking, their feelings, their suffering, their hopes and fears, their successes and failures. Becoming one flesh means that two persons become completely one in body, soul, and spirit and yet remain two different persons.

Goals:

1. To explore biblical concepts and teachings regarding the institution of marriage

2. To share whatever insights that result from the group's examination of the Scriptures

Bible background: Read the following verses:

Genesis 1:26–28; 2:18–24; 5:1–2
Matthew 19:3–12
1 Corinthians 7:2, 28, 39
2 Corinthians 6:14–18
Ephesians 5:21–31
1 Timothy 5:14
Hebrews 13:4

Group exercises: Definitions of Marriage

1. Depending on the size of the group, you may wish to divide it into smaller groups (of four or five) and assign one or two of the scriptural passages to each group. Following the reading of these scriptural passages, ask each group to come up with a definition of marriage based on the portion of Scripture they read.

2. As the leader, direct the group in a discussion of Genesis 2:24.

a. What is implied in the phrase "leaving father and mother"?

b. What is the meaning of the word "cleave" (in the KJV)?

c. What is meant by the phrase "become one flesh"?

3. Discuss with the entire group their understanding of Genesis 1:27–28 and 5:1–2.

   a. Point out to the group how both passages deal with the male and female being created equally.

   b. As the leader, you will probably want to do some research on the meaning of the words *Adam, Eve, man,* and *woman.* Be willing to share with the group whatever insights you have gained from your research.

   c. Share the following questions with the group:

   • In what ways are men and women the same?

   • In what ways are they different?

   • Does the Bible affirm the equality of the sexes or the inequality of the sexes?

   • What qualities do men admire most in women?

   • What qualities do women admire most in men?

Closing exercise:

Ask each person to write on a piece of paper three things they admire in their spouse and three things they admire about themselves. Allow couples to exchange their responses with each other and discuss them. (For comparative purposes only, they can match their responses to the statement "Things I admire about myself" with the responses of their spouse.)

Session 2: "Rebellion, Ruin, and Reconciliation"

Time: 1 1/2 hours

Materials needed: Bibles, flip chart, pencils, paper

Reflections: One of the characteristics of adolescence is reflected in changing family relationships. Many parents and teenagers fear adolescence because they equate changed relationships with alienation. On the other hand, for some families, the teen years are the closest and best.

Goal: To gain biblical insights and understanding about conflicts that arise in families

Bible background: Read the following Bible verses:

Genesis 27:11–36; 33:8–11

Luke 15:11–32

Group exercises:

1. Read the above passages, or have someone in the group do the reading. After the passages have been read, share some of the highlights from the two passages. For example:

   a. Both Jacob and the prodigal son operated out of a mode of self-interest.

   b. Jacob and the prodigal son caused resentment and grief among family members.

   c. Both Jacob and the prodigal son repented of their misdeeds.

   d. Each learned some costly lessons from his indiscreet and intemperate behavior.

   (Note: At this point, do not attempt to engage in a lengthy exposition on the above points. Just briefly introduce them to provoke some thoughts from the group.)

2. Divide your group in half. One group will deal with the passages in Genesis on Esau and Jacob, and the other group will deal with the passage on the prodigal son. If the two groups are extremely large, you will need to divide them into even smaller groups of from 10 to 12. Keep in mind, however, that the additional smaller groups will also discuss one or the other assigned passage.

   Ask the groups to complete the following statements:

   a. When I think of Jacob/prodigal son, I think of . . .

   b. In this story I really feel sorry for . . .

   c. If I had been the prodigal son/Jacob, I would have . . .

   d. If I had been the elder brother/Esau, I think I would have . . .

   e. The following things really speak to me in this story: . . .

   Allow time for the groups to share some of the thoughts and opinions that were generated from this activity within their small group and then the larger group.

3. Distribute blank sheets of paper to the entire group. Ask them to write the names (or some kind of symbol) of three or four persons with whom they have had personal conflict, whom they have been hurt by, or who they have had negative feelings about. Have the group respond to the following questions after they've written down their list of names:

   a. In what way(s) did this person hurt me?

   b. For what reason did this person hurt me?

   c. Did I tell this person I was hurt by his or her words or deeds?

   d. Did I pray for this person and for myself, that our differences would be resolved?

   e. Have I forgiven this person for hurting me?

Keep in mind that this is not an easy activity for persons to participate in. Therefore, you will not want to coerce those members of the group who feel uncomfortable doing this exercise. Following the exercise, you may wish to allow some persons to talk about the difficulty they had in making up a list and responding to the questions. Allow ample time for persons to express what they have learned from this experience.

Closing exercise: Conclude this session by reading the following verses: Matthew 5:23–24 and 18:15–17 and Ephesians 4:26, 31–32. Offer a closing prayer on behalf of the members of the group, or ask several volunteers to offer brief prayers.

Session 3: "Building Self-Esteem among Family Members"

Time: 1 1/2 hours

Materials needed: Bible, chalk, chalkboard, pencils, paper

Reflection: What comes to your mind when you think of the word "esteem"? Consider such ideas as valuing the worth of another person, thinking well of ourselves, or showing respect or appreciation for others.

Goals:

1. To develop deeper interpersonal relationships among church and family members

2. To discover insights from the Bible to build self-esteem in self and in others

Bible background: Read the following Bible verses:

Ephesians 4:25–32

Philippians 4:8

Colossians 3:8–14

Group exercises:

1. Allow about 20 minutes in small groups of five or six for participants to read and discuss the meanings and spiritual implications of the three passages of Scripture in reference to building esteem in the church and family. Be sure to assign to each group one of the Scripture passages. If you have more than three groups, it is all right to assign the same passage more than once.

2. Following the small group discussions, draw a vertical line in the center of the chalkboard or on a large sheet of newsprint with "Church" on the left side and "Family" on the right side. Ask the groups to share some of their thoughts on building esteem in the church and in the family. Discuss some of the thoughts shared by the groups where these are appropriate.

3. Ask each person to write the names of the members of their family on a sheet of paper. They are then to write three things they like about each family member whose name they have written down. (Note: Instruct the members of your group that they are not to mention anything negative about any family member. Only the positive things they like about each person should appear on their sheet.)

Closing exercise: Ask the groups to rearrange themselves into their original small groups. They are then to look at the passages the group had originally studied, but this time they are to write a list of Ten Commandments for Family Relationships. Portions from these lists can be shared with the larger group. You could assign a committee to choose the best 10 of the Ten Commandments to present to the entire group at your next meeting.

End this session by offering prayer for the families comprising your group or by reading the 13th chapter of 1 Corinthians.

Session 4: "Families That Pray Together . . ."

Time: 1 1/2 hrs

Materials needed: Chalk, chalkboard, pencils, paper, church hymnal

Reflection: Just as oxygen sustains the human body, prayer supports the Christian family. Prayer is the flow of energy that enables families to cope with crisis, live in harmony, comfort those who are restless, and encourage those who are disheartened. Talking to God through the medium of prayer is a step that moves families toward maturity in Christ and love toward each other. It has been proven that families who *pray* for each other seldom *prey* on each other.

Goals:

1. To gain an appreciation of the meaning of family prayer
2. To enrich one's personal spiritual life through the exercise of prayer

Bible background: Read the following verses:

Exodus 33:12–17; 10:46–51

2 Chronicles 7:14

Luke 18:1–8

Group Exercises:

1. Divide the large group into four smaller groups and assign one of the passages on prayer to each group. Following the reading of the passage, each group should come up with a definition of prayer. Caution each group to make their definition complete but not too long. Then ask each group to share their definitions with the other groups. In a positive, pleasant way, point out any similarities or differences among the prayer definitions.

2. Ask the groups to reflect on persons they know who are hurting and in need of prayer. Encourage each group to share one or two names from their list of hurting persons. The groups could take turns praying for each other's requests. If there are members of the church family who need prayer, be sure to include them also.

3. Ask family members (nuclear or extended) to form small circles and pair off with another family member (father-daughter, mother-son, brother-sister, uncle-nephew, etc.). Have them share a personal prayer concern with each other and have each family member pray for the other.

Closing exercise: As a final activity, ask the group to list the characteristics of prayer in the following acrostic:

Example:

P _____ Power

R _____ Refreshing

A _____ Agonize

Y _____ Yield

E _____ Examine

R _____ Renewal

Allow for a brief discussion on the words that were generated from the prayer acrostic and conclude with the hymn "What a Friend We Have in Jesus."

The purpose of this chapter was to present practical ways to strengthen marriages and family members in a teaching-learning setting. In our society, the family unit is under attack and family values are eroding all around us. The Christian church has a spiritual mandate to make families whole. These sessions are designed to bring about such transformation.

PART V:

CHRISTIAN EDUCATION AND VALUES

CHAPTER 11

AN OVERVIEW OF CHRISTIAN VALUES

What is a value? A value is a quality of life that drives us to act, or respond, in relationship to a system of beliefs. Our values are therefore rooted in a set of social, religious, political, philosophical, educational, and psychological assumptions that we have made about life. These assumptions are beliefs we have accepted about our work, family, church, faith, and other human relationships that order our lives. (Christian values are similar to general values, but there are some exceptions to be considered. We will concentrate on Christian values in the next chapter and on general values in this one.)

Closely related to our assumptions and beliefs about values are the paths that lead to choices. In fact, choices are the compilation of the assumptions and beliefs that motivate our values, for what we have assumed and believed as valuable will impel our choices. Our choices fall into two categories: (1) those choices that we have internalized and that move us to act when we are confronted with external and internal stimuli; and (2) those choices that we do not consider as an immediate priority but to which we may aspire in the future. Dr. Dennis Deaton writes,

> Our conscious mind possesses a prominent spiritual-moral value system. It wrestles constantly with the issues of "good and bad, right and wrong, workable and unworkable. In contrast to the conscious mind, the subconscious mind does not grapple with the concept of right and wrong, feasible and infeasible in the same way the conscious mind does. The subconscious mind is valueless, immoral or amoral. . . . It is the conscious mind that exerts sovereign control and has full sway [over the conscious mind].[1]

Therefore, the conscious mind is the instigator of behavior, and the subconscious mind functions as the implementer of choices made by our conscious mind. It then follows that bad choices yield bad consequences and good choices yield good consequences.

The ancient wisdom from the writer of Proverbs sums up the powerful way in which we are influenced by our thoughts: "For as [a person] thinks in his heart, so is he" (Proverbs 23:7, NKJV).

VALUES AND CHOICES

Brian P. Hall believes that the underlying process of valuing and setting priorities can be summarized as follows:

1. The assumptions I have about life and living internally will determine the way I behave externally.
2. My behavior reflects my values, i.e. the things I believe to be true and am willing to act upon.[2]

Meanwhile, in their classic work *Values Clarification,* Simon and Kirchenbaum outline the valuing process in the following manner:

1. A value is something I choose freely from among several options with which I am faced.
2. A value is a choice whose built-in consequences I fully realize upon making that choice.
3. A value is something that I willfully and freely choose, without being coerced.
4. A value is an act I cherish and am willing to put my faith in.
5. A value is something I am willing to openly and boldly testify about to others.
6. A value is something I am willing to act upon by spending time on it, giving attention to it, and supporting it in whatever way I can.
7. A value is a pattern of behavior I am willing to repeat over and over again.[3]

Thus a value is the foundation upon which one's behavior is executed. A value is never accidental or incidental, although it can certainly be influenced by a number of sources external to it. Values are the result of deliberate choices, with a realization of the consequences of what one chooses. Furthermore, a value is something one cherishes faithfully and acts upon repeatedly on the basis of what one has chosen freely.

Let us now take a look at some of the factors that have shaped the values of adults, teachers, and leaders.

INFLUENCES THAT HAVE
SHAPED OUR VALUES

Many kinds of influences affect the development of our values, but four are arguably the most important influences for most people: the church, the family, the school, and mass media.

1. **The church.** For Christians, the church is a major influence in the formation of values. In church we learn how to express our love to God, enhance our relationship to Jesus Christ, and consecrate our lives to the indwelling of the Holy Spirit. Moreover, the church is the place where we learn to value having relationships and fellowship with other Christians as well as living in peace and harmony with one another. In a similar fashion, the church is where we learn to value the Bible, God's Word, as the guiding principles and authority for living the Christian life. Through the preaching and teaching of the church, we learn to value truth and enlarge our understanding of God's will for our lives.

2. **The family.** Our parents influence our social, religious, educational, political, and philosophical values. Parental influence can have a positive or negative impact in the formation of values, depending on the quality of the values our parents seek to instill in us. Adults who have been taught values contrary to the teachings of the Bible will need to undergo some radical spiritual conversions before they are ready to affirm the Christian faith.

In many Black families, persons have grown up in homes where there was no live-in father. They have lived in neighborhoods and communities where crime, drugs, gangs, and violence are common. All of these outside forces can also affect family life and values.

For those who teach in the Black church, it is imperative to remember that, even though a person has accepted Christ as personal Savior, he or she still needs to learn biblical principles. Valuing requires a process that takes place over a lengthy period of time. So we must teach positive Christian values to replace those negative values learned previously in the family.

3. **The school.** School helps mold our minds, shape our attitudes, and determine our worldview. Indeed, next to the home, the school holds the most prominent place in many people's lives. In school we are introduced to our heroes and "sheroes." We learn what events are important by studying history. We view our teachers as authority figures, the embodiment of knowledge and truth. The school also expects us to live by its standards and by the subject matter we have been taught. We excel or fail on the basis of how we respond to what we have been taught.

Whether people have been taught in a public or a parochial school, the educational, social, and philosophical values of their school will have a lasting effect on their way of thinking and behaving. Thus it is important to get to know something about how the adults in your class have been impacted by the school system. The college professor or the public school teacher may have been far more influential than the pastor or Sunday School teacher. But this does not mean that you cannot help reshape values in a more positive direction.

It is because education is a lifelong experience that attitudes and values are critical in the teaching and learning process.

4. **Mass media.** Television, radio, newspapers, magazines, computers, the Internet, and other forms of mass communication captivate our minds and dominate our thinking. In a matter of minutes we are bombarded by news and information from around the globe. And our exposure to these sources of information is nearly constant and highly influential. For example, in his book *God's Vision or Television?* Dr. Carl Jeffery Wright makes this stunning statement:

Television is influential. In the United States, it is the main thing we do—and we do it a lot. The average American sits in front of the screen watching TV about 20 hours per week. As Americans we are different for many reasons, but the habitual viewing influence of television is probably what separates us from most of the people in the world today. We rely on television for our vision. Unfortunately, this vision, or televised lifestyle, includes far more violence, drugs, sex and vulgar language than most people would care to see expressed to our youth [and adults].[4]

John Naisbitt told us more than two decades ago that the information society was upon us. Here are some of the key points he discussed in his book Megatrends:

1. The information society is an economic reality. We have moved from an industrial society to an information society.

2. Innovations in communication and computer technology will accelerate the pace of change by collapsing the information flow.

3. We are drowning in information but starved for knowledge. The personal computer explosion is upon us. Furthermore, the innovation of technology has brought us an abundance of information in, for example, biotechnology and genetic engineering.[5] Scientists are now able to alter the genetic code and to clone sheep and other animals. Who knows what else the future of technology may hold? Without a doubt, God is still all knowing and in control of His world. The new technology does, however, raise some concerns when one reflects on how this technology and information will affect what the masses will value now and in the future.

The future of Christian education and the way we will approach teaching will require creative ideas and methods in a changing world. It is imperative that we be aware of how values emerge and are affected by science, technology, and other sources.

CHAPTER 12

IDENTIFYING CORE CHRISTIAN VALUES

Along with the general values that are available for adoption, there are also Christian values. It is important to understand two points that make Christian values distinct. First, Christian values ideally are rooted in Bible truth and validated by belief in Jesus Christ. Second, Christian values are motivated by the Holy Spirit and cause us to behave in accordance with God's will.

Not only can individuals have Christian values; so can organizations, such as churches or Sunday Schools. When we look at the subject of Christian education within the African American context, we must consider what values our educational ministries ought to possess. More particularly, in this final chapter, we will discuss core values and how they work in the context of Christian organizations and churches.

CORE VALUES

Our Christian core values are constant values in our lives and are emotionally charged with convictions that are based in the Bible. Core values influence our decisions, drive our ministry, and direct our behavior. These values are the non-negotiable motivators that describe the essence of an organization or an individual.

Core values may take on the following characteristics:

1. They are consistent and remain in place during the lifetime of an organization. From time to time, they may be amended, but the basic content remains the same.

2. They create excitement, coupled with a keen sense of intellectual investment that generates enthusiasm and energy. Core values light the fire in one's heart

and motivate a person to share that fire with others.

3. They describe the essence of the business a person is in or the organization's reason for being. In the church they must be biblically grounded and contain principles that are true to the values found in scriptural teachings.

4. They influence how an organization makes its decisions. They are ingrained in the mental, social, and spiritual fabric of an organization, so that the organization behaves in a unified fashion in response to those values.

5. Because they have been shared and accepted by an organization, its members are able to move in concert toward common goals.

6. They bring about behavioral change in an organization that will be exercised through consistent actions of its members. Ideally, their "walk" and "talk" are compatible with each other.

CHRISTIAN EDUCATION
AND CORE VALUES

It would be worthwhile for all churches to develop a set of core values for their educational ministries. Core values allow congregations to identify and prioritize the essential qualities that undergird the reasons why their organization exists and the factors that govern what they teach.

Has your church developed a set of core values? How did you go about organizing, planning, and selecting your list of values? What are some of the non-negotiable values that will stand the test of time? Remember, core values must be consistent and emotionally laden and must define the reason why the ministry or program exists. They should also state explicitly how the members act out these values in their daily lives.

Permit me to suggest a list of areas in which you may wish to develop some core values. Keep in mind that I am not suggesting you try to develop core values in all the areas I have listed below. And at the same time, there might be other areas, not listed below, where you may wish to add core values.

God (Father, Son, Holy Spirit)   Family
Church   The world
Bible   Leadership

People (saved and unsaved)	Sin
Evangelism/ministry	Justice
Christian nurture	The soul
Love	Salvation
Lifestyle	Sanctification
Faith	Racism
Stewardship	Truth
Adulthood	Prayer

Before the leaders of your church organization decide to draw from the list of items shown above, you should first try to identify the core values you already share in Christian education. As you formulate your core values, keep in mind that a core value should be biblical and passionate, thus driving your ministry.

Try to sort out personal values as distinct from the core values of your church organization. Keep in mind that a core value is not an opinion of one person or of a group of persons in the church. A value is more than a tradition that has not been tested in the light of scriptural truth. It is a lasting, Bible-based conviction that energizes the people in your organization.

Aubrey Malphurs has identified seven criteria for testing a good value.[1] These criteria can be useful to Christian educators and pastors who want to examine core values for educational ministries.

1. **Is it biblical?** How does a particular value line up with the teaching and doctrines found in the Bible? Can the value be supported by more than a single verse found in the Bible?

2. **Does it engender passion?** A valid witness of God's love and truth from the Bible should generate the fire of excitement and create enthusiasm. And yet a value should do more than just stir the emotions and stick in the memory; it must be inspirational to members of the organization, compelling them to take action.

3. **Is it a shared value?** In what ways do people agree about and hold to the same value? These are essential questions with regard to values. In the valuing process, people must rally around a common cause or basic truth. It is something

that people can participate in together in a spirit of unity and cooperation. Do they enjoy what they are doing and experience a sense of significance and accomplishment while pursuing and practicing that value?

4. **Is it constant?** For values to have lasting and fundamental consequences there must be longevity attached to them. Values should not be temporary and crisis oriented if they are to stand the test of time. Malphurs asks, "Will this value stand the test of time? More importantly, will people strive to live for this value twenty-five, fifty, or even one hundred years from now? In a time of accelerating, cataclysmic change core values must remain intact."[2]

5. **Can it be expressed clearly?** A good value is never fuzzy or hazy—it must be clear to all who will use it. If your presentation is not clear to you, it will not be clear to the people to whom you are giving it. God said to Habakkuk, "Write the vision and make it plain" (Habakkuk 2:2, NKJV). "If those who select an organization's values are not clear on them, then those within that organization who are expected to embrace those values will be lost."[3]

6. **Is it congruent with other values?** Value conflict often occurs in church organizations, and more often than not, these conflicts are rooted in differences about what is a core value. A case in point is the challenge of starting a ministry to homeless people. The problem surfaces when the homeless are invited to be a part of the 11 a.m. Sunday service. They may not be properly dressed (according to some of the upscale members), or they may not smell like they have just stepped out of a bubble bath, and so not everyone is in agreement that these people really ought to be present in the church service. Values are not congruent when our talk does not line up with our walk.

7. **Can it be implemented?** A value that is not workable is a liability, not an asset. The church must be of one accord on values that are to be implemented. In short, there must be buy-in to the values being proposed. Or to put it another way, the people must be in the airplane on the takeoff if you want them to be with you on the landing. Whenever there is a stalemate, a holdup, or a shutdown in an organization, it is usually a matter of faulty implementation.

Teaching for values. Neither Christian nor secular educational institutions are values free. Being educators, we have an agenda we are trying to get across to our students. In the case of Christian educators, what we present is (hopefully) biblically based and spiritually correct. Fortunately, God is not democratic. Neither is the Bible tolerant of those who do not love the truth. And so Christian teachers, seeking to represent God faithfully, are on a mission. Our mission is to change lives by the means and methods outlined in the Bible—our Book of values.

Our mandate has been clear from the beginning of the New Testament church. We are to "go and make disciples of all nations, baptizing them in the name of the Father and of the Son and of the Holy Spirit, and teaching them to obey everything I [Jesus] have commanded you" (Matthew 28:18–20, NIV). Jesus also said, "You will be my witnesses in Jerusalem, and in all Judea and Samaria, and to the ends of the earth" (Acts 1:8, NIV).

Know your own values. In order to be a good teacher of values, it is necessary for you to know what values are important to you. Knowing your core values will assist you to help your adult learners develop and evaluate their own values.

Make a list of some of the core values you strongly believe in. Then rank the values on a scale of 1 to 3, with 1 being the highest priority. After each value has received its priority ranking of 1, 2, or 3, respond to the following questions.

	Yes	No	Not Sure
1. Is this a value I am willing to live for?	____	____	____
2. Is this a value I will not compromise?	____	____	____
3. Is this a value for which I am willing to accept the consequences for embracing it?	____	____	____
4. Is this a value I am willing to spend time, energy, and money to support?	____	____	____
5. Is this a value that can be supported by teachings of the Bible and will contribute to my spiritual growth?	____	____	____
6. Is this a value I am willing to openly and freely share with others?	____	____	____
7. Is this a value I comprehend enough so that I can clearly teach it to the adults in my class?	____	____	____
8. Is this a value the African American learners in my class would find helpful?	____	____	____
9. Is this a value that brings glory to God?	____	____	____
10. If others saw me practicing this value, would I continue to practice it?	____	____	____

COVENANT, COMMITMENTS, AND AFFIRMATIONS OF CHRISTIAN VALUES

The covenant, commitments, and affirmations that follow are intended to show how congregations and Christian education boards or committees can draft value statements to unify their congregation and its organizations. These statements are only illustrative of how value statements should look and they are by no means absolute. I urge each congregation or Christian education board to develop its own list of values.

The following pages contain an example of the components of a value covenant.

The Covenant of Values for Church Membership

Because I believe that I have been led by the Spirit of God to become a member of _____ [church name], I willingly commit and freely accept the values outlined in the following covenant:

1. I covenant to live in accordance with the New Testament teachings concerning faith in Jesus Christ, love for God the Father, and obedience to the Holy Spirit.

2. I covenant to live a Spirit-filled and Spirit-led life of practical holiness so that no reproach is brought upon my church.

3. I covenant to practice the following ordinances of _____ _____ [church name]: baptism by immersion, regular participation in Holy Communion, and the observance of foot washing.

4. I covenant to be faithful in attendance at worship, to support the pastoral and spiritual leadership of the church, and to pray for the pastor and other leaders of the church.

5. I covenant to happily engage in the work of the church by seeking to discover my spiritual gifts and how I may use these gifts in the work of the Lord.

6. I covenant to love the members of this church, seeking to edify and strengthen them, and refuse to engage in gossiping, backbiting, or willfully engaging in unChristian behavior concerning members of the church or other persons.

7. I covenant to refrain from all sexual immorality and the use of illicit drugs, alcohol, and tobacco, recognizing that my body is the temple of the Holy Spirit.

8. I covenant to participate in holy and spiritual activities that will enhance my Christian life and character. These activities include regular worship and celebration of Christ, midweek Bible study, prayer and fasting, daily Bible reading, quiet times of meditation before the Lord, the reading of good books, and witness to others.

9. I covenant to pray for the members of _____ [church name], demonstrate love and concern for them, rejoice and celebrate in their accomplishments, and be willing to assist them in times of stress, sorrow, suffering, and spiritual need.

10. I covenant to support my church with tithes and offerings, recognizing that I am to be a good steward of all God has entrusted to me.

Signature:_____ Date:_____

Commitment to Leadership Values

Because I have accepted a position of leadership and trust from the pastor and members of this church, _____ [church name], I affirm that the following statements are true.

1. I have received Christ as my personal Savior and Lord of my life and have been baptized in water in the name of the Father, Son, and Holy Spirit.

2. I have accepted the leading and guiding of God's Holy Spirit in my life, and I am striving to walk daily in His Spirit by pursuing holiness as a lifestyle.

3. I will attend regular worship services and Bible study, training classes, cell meetings, and other special services held at this church.

4. I am committed to the family of believers that gather at _____ _____ [church name], _____ _____ [address, city, state], and will pray for them, live in harmony with them, and worship and work consistently with them, according to the leading of the Holy Spirit.

5. I accept the leadership of the pastor and other chosen and appointed leaders of _____ [church name] and agree to pray for and work with them in a cooperative and Christian manner.

6. I will faithfully carry out the duties and responsibilities I have accepted, and in those instances where I am not able to do so, I will inform the pastor (or those designated by the pastor) of my inability to serve or attend the event.

7. I will faithfully present my tithes and give my offerings to this church, recognizing that I am only a steward of the resources God has entrusted to me.

Signature:_____ Date:_____

Commitment to Bible Values and Christian Conduct

Having been led by the Spirit of God to receive the Lord Jesus Christ as personal Savior, and on the profession of our faith having been baptized in the name of the Father and of the Son and of the Holy Spirit, we do now in the presence of God and this assembly most solemnly and joyfully enter into covenant with one another as one body of Christ.

A. Biblical Values Concerning Our Church

We engage, therefore, by the aid of the Holy Spirit, to do the following:

1. Walk together in Christian love (John 13:34–35)

2. Strive for the advancement of this church in knowledge, holiness, and comfort (Ephesians 4:3; 2 Timothy 2:15)

3. Promote its prosperity and spirituality (2 Corinthians 7:1; Philippians 1:27)

4. Sustain its worship, ordinances, discipline, and doctrines (Matthew 28:19; 1 Corinthians 11:23–26; Hebrews 10:25; Jude 3)

B. Biblical Values Concerning Our Stewardship

We will contribute cheerfully and regularly to the following:

1. The support of the ministry (1 Corinthians 16:2; 2 Corinthians 8:6–7)

2. The expenses of the church (Malachi 3:8–10)

3. The relief of the poor (Matthew 25:34–40)

4. And the spread of the gospel through all nations (Matthew 28:19–20; Acts 1:8)

C. Biblical Values Concerning Our Homes

We endeavor to do the following at home:

1. Maintain family and secret devotions (Acts 7:11; 1 Thessalonians 5:17–18)

2. Religiously educate our children (Deuteronomy 6:4–7; Ephesians 6:1–4; 2 Timothy 3:15)

3. Seek the salvation of our kindred and acquaintances (Proverbs 11:30; Matthew 4:19; Acts 1:8)

D. Biblical Values Concerning Our Conduct

We will endeavor to conduct our lives in the following manner:

1. Live a moral and ethical life (Ephesians 5:15–21; 2 Peter 3:11)

2. Be just in our dealings (Romans 12:17)

3. Be faithful in our commitment (Romans 13:8; Revelation 2:10)

4. Be exemplary in our conduct (Romans 14:13; 1 John 2:10)

5. Avoid all tattling, backbiting, and excessive anger (Proverbs 26:20; Ephesians 4:31; Colossians 3:8; James 3:1–2; 1 Peter 2:21–23)

6. Abstain from the sale and use of intoxicating drinks, drugs, and other such substances (Proverbs 20:1; Habakkuk 2:15; Ephesians 5:16–18)

7. Be enthusiastic in our efforts to advance the kingdom of our Savior (Ephesians 2:10; Titus 2:14; 3:8)

E. Biblical Values Concerning Our Relationships with Church Members

We promise to do the following:

1. Watch over each other in brotherly love (Philippians 2:4; 1 Peter 1:22)

2. Remember each other in prayer (James 5:16)

3. Aid each other in sickness and distress (Galatians 6:2; James 2:14–17)

4. Cultivate Christian sympathy in feeling and Christian courtesy in speech (1 Peter 3:8–11)

5. Be slow to be offended but always be ready for reconciliation, remembering the rules of our Savior to secure peace without delay (Matthew 5:23–24; 18:15–17; Ephesians 4:30–32)

An Affirmation of My Faith and Values

This is your testament of faith and the core values that you are convinced are the driving principles of your life. Complete the following statements, take some quiet time to contemplate them, share them with your pastor or a close friend, place them among your important records, and request that they be read at your funeral.

I believe in the following values . . .

1.

2.

3.

I am convinced that these values . . .

1.

2.

3.

It is because of these values that my life is greatly enriched by . . .

1.

2.

3.

I could live without some things, but I could not live without . . .

1.

2.

3.

I want those who know me to realize that . . .

1.

2.

3.

Signature: _____ Date: _____

PART VI:

17 METHODS TO ENERGIZE YOUR SUNDAY SCHOOL STAFF AND PROGRAMS

17 METHODS TO ENERGIZE YOUR
SUNDAY SCHOOL STAFF AND PROGRAMS

For a vast majority of African American churches, the Sunday School is still the primary vehicle for Christian education. This is especially true in rural settings and for a large number of Black congregations in the South. Perhaps for some years to come, this situation in Christian education will continue to exist. This is probably true for at least three reasons: (1) there are many pastors who preside at more than one church; (2) many pastors do not live in the community where the church is located; and (3) regular worship service with preaching is held only once or twice monthly. Therefore, Sunday School, for many churches, is an alternative to the morning worship service.

Nevertheless, there is a significant number of African American churches where new methods have been employed and Christian education programs have replaced the Sunday School. Still others have augmented the traditional adult Sunday School in the sanctuary by going beyond the single teacher and arranging theater-type classrooms with team teachers. Adult classes in some of the more innovative churches now meet on Saturday or Sunday afternoon, while others have chosen to meet on weeknights. During the adult class time, children and youth meet as separate groups.

For those churches who have embraced a cell group model, the Sunday School has been replaced by an intimate group consisting of 12 to 15 people. Often these cell groups meet for fellowship, Bible study, intercessory prayer, and personal testimony time. In a growing number of such congregations, elective courses are also offered. Marriage, conflict resolution, leadership, specific Bible subjects, and spiritual gifts are some of the topics taught and discussed.

An effort to adapt Christian education to current conditions in Black churches is an extremely worthwhile endeavor. However, as mentioned previously, the traditional Sunday School remains dominant in Christian education among African American congregations. And so, in the pages that follow, I am submitting some of the ways the traditional Sunday School can be strengthened in African American churches. It is my belief that a well-functioning Sunday School can lead to church growth and quality Christian education.

For those churches who still view the Sunday School as their primary method of Christian education for children, youth and adults, here are 17 ways for churches to energize their Sunday School:

1. Know the mission of the church and the church school.
2. Work toward an ABC plan.
3. Elevate the Sunday School through careful planning.
4. Launch a new Sunday School year.
5. Achieve the 12 steps and strengthen the Sunday School.
6. Evaluate your Sunday School.
7. Check your self and spiritual awareness.
8. Complete a workers' needs checklist.
9. Hold a special meeting for teachers.
10. Know and understand your students.
11. Find quality adult Sunday School leaders and teachers.
12. Celebrate the Sunday School through special events.
13. Strengthen and support the Sunday School as a pastor.
14. Consider implementing these Sunday School classes.
15. Ask yourself, Am I an exciting teacher?
16. Use a job description for the Sunday School superintendent.
17. Conduct an overview of your Sunday School program.

CHAPTER 13

ENERGIZING METHODS 1 THROUGH 4

Method 1: Know the Mission of the Church and the Church School

The aim of the following work sheet is to guide local church leaders in exploring the mission of the church and of the Sunday School. The pastor, associate ministers, members of the board of Christian education and church council, Sunday School superintendent, and other key leaders should plan a special session to use this work sheet.

Outline:

I.   Why does the church exist? What is the church's mission?

II. Why is the Sunday School important?

III. What are some ways to help members and leaders of a local congregation be more conscious of the church's mission and the purpose of the Sunday School?

Process:

I.   Why does the church exist? What is the church's mission? List the two questions above on newsprint or chalkboard.

A. Read and discuss Matthew 28:19–20, Acts 1:8, 1 Peter 2:9–10, and 1 John 4:7–21.

B. Ask each individual to think about and jot down keywords and ideas that express his or her hope for the church.

C. Share thoughts and write key ideas on chalkboard or newsprint.

D. Distribute copies of the "Purpose for Christian Education" statement that has been formulated by the director and board of Christian education. Study it individually, then discuss it in small groups.

E. In groups of two or three, write a mission statement for your congregation. Each group should write on newsprint and tape it to the wall.

II. What is the purpose and mission of the Sunday School? Write this question on chalkboard or newsprint.

A. Read and discuss Romans 10:14–17 as well as Ephesians 2:19–22 and 4:1–7, 11–16.

B. Individually write ideas and keywords that come to mind in response to the question on chalkboard.

C. Share ideas with the entire group or in small groups and write key ideas and words on chalkboard or newsprint.

D. Work in small groups to formulate a common statement of purpose for the Sunday School. Put these statements on newsprint and post them on walls around room.

III. Ways to help leaders and members of your local congregation become more conscious of the mission of the church and the Sunday School

A. Share and discuss discoveries made about the purpose of the church and the Sunday School.

B. Brainstorm and list ideas for helping the whole church become more aware of its mission. Think of all the different age groups, organizations, classes, and fellowship groups in the church. Zero in on implications for the ministry of your congregation.

C. Close the session with a time of quietness to reflect on discoveries made about the church's mission. Pray that the whole congregation may become more conscious of its mission and more active in carrying it out.[1]

Method 2: Work Toward an ABC Plan

The outline below is an illustration to help your Christian education committee or board to brainstorm some creative ideas and a plan of action for teaching a Bible lesson.

Give each member of your planning committee or board a copy of the following form. Ask each person to identify the specific needs and concerns under item A. Follow a similar procedure for letters B and C. Allow 30 to 45 minutes for the entire exercise. Be sure to go through each of the three steps to develop the fundamentals of a lesson plan.

Planning Form

A. Identify needs and concerns.

Special concerns of age level: _____

_____

Specific needs and concerns of individual persons: _____

_____

Specific concerns lifted up in Bible passages and curriculum materials: _____

_____

_____

B. Decide what actions you will take.

Desired outcome: _____

_____

Ideas and activities to consider: _____

_____

_____

Plan of action: (Do a more detailed plan on separate sheets.)

1. Scripture to be used: _____
2. How you will begin: _____
3. Learning activities: _____

_____

4. How you will close: _____

_____

5. Special preparation and arrangements: _____

_____

_____

C. Check up and evaluate.

1. How session progressed: _____
2. What was accomplished: _____

_____

_____

3. Who and what needs further attention for next week:[2] _____

_____

_____

Method 3: Elevate the Sunday School through Creative Planning

I. Be sure the Sunday School is getting its share of planning time and energy.

The Sunday School is the most successful ongoing volunteer enterprise in most of our communities and certainly in the church. Many Sunday Schools have at least six or eight persons who have planned, prepared, and are ready to teach one or more other persons every Sunday morning. The Sunday School appears to go on without committed effort, and sometimes it does. For the most part, the Sunday School continues because there are persons who care and pray and quietly do their work week after week. But the Sunday School needs attention—planning attention—if it is to be effective.

Local boards often have many items of concern to deal with at each meeting. It is quite easy for a board of Christian education to do everything else on its agenda, with the Sunday School superintendent spending all of the time on Sunday-by-Sunday operation problems and not giving the Sunday School the kind of quality planning it really needs. The result is that the Sunday School is not discussed or planned at any length by the local church board of Christian education.

II. Give the Sunday School its due in the board of Christian education planning time, or consider appointing a special Sunday church school planning committee. Such a committee could include the Sunday School superintendent plus two or three other persons. This committee would be accountable to the board of Christian education but would give the Sunday School more of the quality time and the energy it needs. Such a committee would set goals, develop strategies for reaching the goals, and frequently evaluate both the planning process and the successes and failures of the Sunday School.

Following is a possible agenda for a board of Christian education meeting focusing on the Sunday School and Christian education programs.

A. Begin with devotion and prayer. Use Ephesians 4:11–16. Invite comments from the group about the significance of this passage before spending time in prayer.

B. Discuss the purpose of this meeting. The purpose might be stated simply as "To build up the Sunday School."

C. Write a purpose statement. Target the statement for the Sunday School in your congregation. Write each of the three following purpose statements on newsprint or chalkboard or possibly type them for duplication.

1. The purpose of the Sunday School is to build up the faith of children, youth, and adults through Bible study, Christian love, acceptance, and caring throughout the week and through prayer for each other.

2. The purpose of the Sunday School is to help children, youth, and adults become more aware of God, respond in faith and love, and become an active part of the body of Christ.

3. The purpose of the Sunday School is to build up the whole church and to help persons know more deeply other persons in the church.

Ask persons to rank these three statements in the order that best describes for them the purpose of the Sunday School in the congregation. Ask persons to share briefly why they rated the purpose statements as they did. Feel free to change these statements and add others appropriate for your Sunday School.

D. List the strength(s) of the Sunday School in your congregation. What identified needs is it currently meeting? What is it doing well? What is the good news about your Sunday School?

E. List the concerns and weaknesses of your Sunday School. What needs to be strengthened? What isn't being done very well? What needs are not being met? What needs to be changed if the Sunday School is going to become what it can in your church and community?

F. Identify the resources in your congregation and community to strengthen the Sunday School. What are the people resources? What are the building and facility resources? What are the financial resources? What are the needs remaining to be met? As these are considered, again check the strengths of the Sunday School in item D above.

G. Brainstorm ideas for strengthening the Sunday School. How can the resources identified in item F be better used to build up the Sunday School? List at least 25 ideas for strengthening the Sunday School and making better use of the resources and opportunities in your congregation and the surrounding community.

III. Examine the quality of the planning being done.

A. Discuss ways that a greater sense of joy might emerge from the planning and service given to the Sunday School.

The late Dr. Donald A. Courtney, Executive Secretary of the Board of Christian Education of the Church of God, identified six basic ingredients for making one's service a joy.

1. A basic belief that the responsibilities you carry for the Sunday School make a difference in the results accomplished

2. Maintaining an attitude that looks at responsibility as challenges rather than as problems

3. The expectation that you as a teacher/worker will grow through the experience of your own work

4. Taking an inward look at yourself and ask in what ways you can improve

5. Prayer for your students

6. Seeking the guidance of the Holy Spirit[3]

B. Consider the strategies needed for recruiting and keeping effective Sunday School teachers. The primary discussion here is to focus on the topic "A Dozen Strategies for Recruiting and Keeping Great Sunday Church School Teachers." See the list of ideas below.

1. Surround yourself with top-quality people.

2. Provide your teachers with a sense of vision.

3. Establish a spirit of unity in the Sunday School department.

4. Identify qualities of success.

5. Recruit students through outreach and evangelism.

6. Nurture potential teachers in advance.

7. Supervise.

8. Train regular and prospective teachers by providing workshops, seminars, and conferences.

9. Give positive reinforcement.

10. Identify hot topics or important psychological needs.

11. Build positive self-esteem in teachers and students.

12. Find positive solutions to help teachers who need to improve their teaching skills.[4]

In your discussion, check three or four of the 12 strategies that your congregation is now doing most effectively. Next, indicate those three or four items your congregation needs to work on most if its recruitment and support efforts for teachers in the Sunday School are going to be truly effective.

The following checklist will help elevate and improve your Sunday School. Use it to evaluate the strengths and weaknesses of your Sunday School department.

Checklist

1.	We begin our Sunday School with devotion and prayer.	❑ Yes ❑ No	❑ Sometimes
2.	We encourage each teacher to spend time in Bible study and lesson planning for their classes.	❑ Yes ❑ No	❑ Sometimes
3.	We have a mission statement for our Sunday School.	❑ Yes ❑ No	❑ Sometimes
4.	We have teachers' meetings on a regular basis.	❑ Yes ❑ No	❑ Sometimes
5.	We encourage our teachers to contact their class members when they are absent two weeks in a row.	❑ Yes ❑ No	❑ Sometimes
6.	Our Sunday School lessons deal with real issues that adults are facing.	❑ Yes ❑ No	❑ Sometimes
7.	We view our Sunday School as an outreach ministry of the church.	❑ Yes ❑ No	❑ Sometimes
8.	Our church's physical facilities are adequate for our Sunday School classes.	❑ Yes ❑ No	❑ Sometimes
9.	Our adult Sunday School teachers have received adequate teacher training.	❑ Yes ❑ No	❑ Sometimes
10.	We seek to recruit new teachers for our Sunday School program.	❑ Yes ❑ No	❑ Sometimes
11.	We have a philosophy in our Sunday School whereby the methods and approaches of teaching adults are extremely different than teaching children and youth.	❑ Yes ❑ No	❑ Sometimes

Method 4: Launch a New Sunday School Year (Checklist)

The checklist on the next page is designed to help local churches start their Sunday School year. It can be a valuable tool to assist your planning group in covering all the areas in launching your Sunday School program. After checking the appropriate Yes or No response, you will want to tabulate the results and spend some time discussing both the Yes and No answers to prioritize what you will cover first.

Stage I: Preparation

1. The work plan of the board of Christian education or a planning committee is in place. ❑ Yes ❑ No

2. We have determined the goals for this year's launch day, including: a) What we expect will happen, b) How many people we hope will attend, c) The kind of attitude we hope to stimulate.

3. We have set a date to launch our Sunday School year. ❑ Yes ❑ No

4. We have decided the activities and events that will be a part of launch day this year: teacher dedication, special program, a picnic or fellowship dinner, etc. ❑ Yes ❑ No

5. We have developed plans for each of the events and appointed committees. ❑ Yes ❑ No

6. We have planned a special meeting for Sunday School teachers and workers to prepare for launch day. (Be sure they are aware of plans and are included in the planning details.) ❑ Yes ❑ No

7. We have communicated to the people who will participate and have considered the following: How will the launch day be publicized? How will the Sunday School teachers and workers be made aware of it? How will the church members—children, youth, and adults—all become aware of it and its importance? How will the entire city and community come to know about launch day? How will people who seldom come to church be notified? How can new persons be informed of this important day in your church? ❑ Yes ❑ No

8. We have set the time for a special teachers' training, "The Art of Caring," or recommended a date to the appropriate planning group. ❑ Yes ❑ No

Stage II: Follow-Through

Preparation is inadequate unless there is proper follow-through. Here are some questions to assist in this process:

1. Are assignments being carried out by individuals and committees? Is the planning getting done on schedule?   ❑ Yes   ❑ No

2. Have announcements appeared in the Sunday bulletin, in the midweek newsletter, in the community newspaper? Are public service announcements on radio and television? Has word come from the pulpit and in Sunday School classes about launch day plans?   ❑ Yes   ❑ No

3. Have Sunday School teachers joined together for inspiration, fellowship, and planning?   ❑ Yes   ❑ No

4. Have teacher-training sessions been planned and publicized?   ❑ Yes   ❑ No

5. Has the pastor been involved in the planning and/or been kept well informed of the plans so that he or she can support the launch day plans?   ❑ Yes   ❑ No

Stage III: Launch Day Ideas

Here are some specific suggestions for launch day:

1. We have kept a spirit of excitement and celebration in all that is done.   ❑ Yes   ❑ No

2. We have honored and acknowledged our teachers by thanking them and praying for them.   ❑ Yes   ❑ No

3. We have two or three people in public worship services—morning and evening—give brief testimonies of what the Sunday School means to them. (A young woman shared recently that her self-worth was greatly affirmed when she started attending a particular Sunday School class in her local church.)   ❑ Yes   ❑ No

4. We have emphasized the importance of the Sunday ❑ Yes ❑ No
    School and of teaching in the church. All that happens
    on launch day should help everybody in the church be-
    lieve the teaching ministry is one of the most important
    ministries performed week after week.

5. We have created a climate of friendliness and caring. ❑ Yes ❑ No
    Help people experience the joy in your church and
    Christian activities. Strive to help everyone who is a
    part of launch day know the special caring that is an
    important aspect of Christian education. Do everything
    possible to help attendees feel at home, welcomed, and
    appreciated.

Stage IV: Follow-Up

End the event well by following up on what took place during launch day.

1. We have evaluated our launch day: a) What were its ❑ Yes ❑ No
    strengths and weaknesses? b) What suggestions should
    be noted for next year?

2. We have listed ways that the spirit and excitement of ❑ Yes ❑ No
    launch day this year can be continued throughout the
    year.

3. We have put in place some kind of launch emphasis ❑ Yes ❑ No
    each quarter.

4. We have made sure teachers and workers have ample ❑ Yes ❑ No
    opportunities for further training and inspiration.
    Teachers should be assured they have the full support of
    your board of Christian education, the pastor, and the
    entire church—not only on launch day but also every
    week throughout the year.

5. We have checked to see that teachers and workers have ❑ Yes ❑ No
    the resources they need, adequate space and equip-
    ment for their classes, and the partnership of the whole
    church in carrying out their important ministry.

CHAPTER 14

ENERGIZING METHODS 5 THROUGH 8

The next four methods can serve as valuable tools to facilitate the Sunday School superintendent, director of Christian education, board of Christian education, planning committee, and Sunday School teacher. Those who will use these methods will gain insights on how to improve their teaching and administrative abilities.

Method 5: Achieve 12 Steps and Strengthen the Sunday School

1. *Recognize* the importance of the teachers and leaders. No Sunday School is better than its leaders and teachers. So encourage the best Sunday School teachers to serve, as poor-quality and poorly motivated teachers kill the spirit of the Sunday School. Expect teachers and leaders to be prepared and to give of their best.

2. *Keep* a strong support system active for all Sunday School leaders and teachers. Minister to the Sunday School leaders and teachers. Make sure that no one serves alone, since we are workers together. Minister to the families of teachers and leaders.

3. *Provide* regular times of training and refreshment for leaders and teachers.

4. *Make* the Sunday School and all of its classes pleasant, relaxed, and enjoyable places for students to learn. The rooms should be clean and appropriately decorated to enhance student focus on Christ-centered improvements.

5. *Use* only the best available Sunday School curriculum materials. Do not settle for what seems easier and simpler, if it is not the best. Invite the board of Christian education, rather than individual teachers, to prayerfully and carefully make curriculum decisions.

6. *Expect* leaders and teachers to care about persons through visits, phone calls, cards, and letters. Consider each class an ICU (intensive care unit).

7. *Minister* to special needs. In every community there are special needs. Minister to challenges among your day care and nursery children, youth, young adults, single persons, young married persons, widowed and divorced adults, parents of teens, midlife adults, and older adults.

8. *Sharpen* leaders' and teachers' understanding of whatever is done. Place emphasis on doing tasks well. Fine-tune leadership activities for maximizing results.

9. *Plan* carefully and give even more attention to carrying out the plans.

10. *Go tell* it on the mountain—with conviction! Promote, publicize, and persuade.

11. *Minister* to the whole person and the family.

12. *Plan* for intergenerational groups. Avoid too much emphasis on age; focus on needs and concerns instead.

Method 6: Evaluate Your Sunday School

Organization	Satisfactory	Needs Improvement
1. The board or committee responsible for the operation of the Sunday School meets at least monthly.	_____	_____
2. All teachers are appointed by the board or committee administering the Sunday School.	_____	_____
3. Teachers meet regularly for lesson planning sessions under the direction of a superintendent or head teacher.	_____	_____
4. A minimum of one hour each week is devoted to the class sessions.	_____	_____
5. An adequate record-keeping system is maintained to identify attendees, absentees, and prospective members.	_____	_____
6. Recognition is given for faithful attendance of at least 46 weeks for a given year.	_____	_____
Leadership Development	Satisfactory	Needs Improvement
1. Each officer and teacher has made a public profession of Christ as Savior and lives in harmony with the teachings of the Bible.	_____	_____
2. A public installation service is held for all teachers and officers in the Sunday School.	_____	_____
3. All teachers and officers attend Sunday morning worship at least three times a month.	_____	_____
4. Sunday School staff meetings are held quarterly with at least 75 percent of staff present.	_____	_____
5. Teacher-training courses are provided for Sunday School staff.	_____	_____
6. Most of the teachers have attended one teacher-training program sponsored by a national Christian education organization.	_____	_____
Curriculum Methods	Satisfactory	Needs Improvement
1. All teachers use the Bible as well as curriculum materials and other teaching aids in their teaching preparation.	_____	_____

(Continued on next page)

Curriculum Methods cont.	Satisfactory	Needs Improvement
2. A board or committee reviews curriculum needs annually and selects the curriculum.		
3. Church curricula are used in most of the classes.	_____	_____
4. At least one elective is provided for adults each quarter.	_____	_____
5. At least one elective course on church doctrine was offered in the past year.	_____	_____
6. New books and/or other resources were added to the church library during this past year.	_____	_____

Facilities and Equipment	Satisfactory	Needs Improvement
1. Adequate space is provided for each class (25 sq. ft. per child; 15 sq. ft. per youth and adult).	_____	_____
2. Classes are separated by partitions.	_____	_____
3. Class settings are clean, well lighted, and attractively decorated.	_____	_____
4. Walls include space for posters, pictures, maps, etc.	_____	_____
5. In each class, furniture is adequate and movable and of the proper size.	_____	_____
6. Chalkboards, maps, CD players, videos, and visual projectors are available to the teachers.	_____	_____

Outreach	Satisfactory	Needs Improvement
1. Specific opportunities are given for students to receive Christ as Savior.	_____	_____
2. Each new student is contacted personally by someone in the Sunday School.	_____	_____
3. A special Sunday School growth program was conducted during the year.	_____	_____
4. An active home or extension department exists for workers to contact persons unable to attend class.	_____	_____
5. At least one course provides discipling for new Christians.	_____	_____
6. There is a visitation evangelism program to help share the faith with friends and acquaintances.	_____	_____

Method 7: Check Your Self and Spiritual Awareness

Values	Of great importance to me	Of some importance to me	Of little or no importance to me
1. I enjoy getting to know the students I teach.			
2. I enjoy getting to know other teachers in our local church.			
3. As a teacher, I have the opportunity to discover new ideas, books, and resources.			
4. Through serving as a teacher, I have the opportunity to learn leadership and communication skills as well as social graces.			
5. As a teacher, I am able to be involved in the lives of others and to share their burdens and concerns, joys and excitements.			
6. I feel honored to be a Sunday School teacher.			
7. I value being known as a caring person by the class I teach and the church I serve.			
8. I experience joy in using the gifts and abilities God has given me.			
9. I am challenged and inspired as I study and prepare for class sessions.			
10. I find a sense of belonging and feel needed in serving as a Sunday School teacher.			
11. I am grateful for the recognition I receive by teaching in the local church.			
12. I feel a sense of importance in being a Sunday School teacher.			
13. I often feel that I am really helping others by being a teacher.			
14. I appreciate the new friendships I have made while serving as a teacher.			
15. Teaching is like a great adventure, and it is exciting to me.			
16. Teaching provides me with an opportunity to change the world and have an influence upon others.			

(Continued on next page)

Values cont.	Of great importance to me	Of some importance to me	Of little or no importance to me
17. By serving as a Sunday School teacher, I am able to further the cause of Christ and His church.	_____	_____	_____
18. As a teacher, I have come to a better understanding of the Bible and of the Christian faith.	_____	_____	_____

Method 8: Complete a Workers' Needs Checklist

Statement of Need	Satisfactorily met at present time	Need help with this need in my life
1. To have a vision of myself as a successful and effective Sunday School teacher	_____	_____
2. To receive appreciation and affirmation from others	_____	_____
3. To be known as a person of worth by others in the church	_____	_____
4. To feel important as a Sunday School teacher and to feel that my work as a teacher is worth it	_____	_____
5. To have a personal relationship with God and to sense that the relationship is growing in depth and meaning	_____	_____
6. To understand the church and my place in it	_____	_____
7. To see God's work as involving our local church, as well as in global outreach through other churches and para-church groups	_____	_____
8. To feel comfortable with my understanding of the Christian faith and my own and my local church's practice of it	_____	_____
9. To know the people who are in my class in sufficient depth	_____	_____
10. To manage my time in such a way that I feel I am in control of it	_____	_____
11. To feel that I have some time of my own and have the choice as to how I use it	_____	_____
12. To be able to relax in private and in the company of others	_____	_____
13. To deal with behavior problems in the class I teach in a Christlike way	_____	_____
14. To experience the personal support of the pastor and other key persons in our local church	_____	_____
15. To know how to prepare a class session that can have real meaning for the people in my class and help me to feel I have been a good teacher	_____	_____
16. To be able to better communicate my feelings, needs, and values to others	_____	_____
17. To be a better listener	_____	_____
18. To enjoy a closer fellowship with workers and leaders in the church	_____	_____

CHAPTER 15

ENERGIZING METHODS 9 THROUGH 14

Method 9: Hold a Special Meeting for Teachers

Purpose: To provide Sunday School teachers and workers with the opportunity to set goals, prepare interesting Sunday School classes, and discuss ways of making new persons feel accepted and welcomed

Setting: A room where persons can be seated comfortably in a circle. Plan for light refreshments and an enjoyable time together. An hour and a half to two hours is needed for this session.

Session Outline:

I.   Begin with a time of prayer and devotions.

II. Share some of the good experiences in Sunday School that have occurred in the past few months.

III. Explore possible goals that each teacher and class might set for the year and the current quarter.

IV. Look at possible ways of reaching new persons and encouraging more regular attendance by current members.

V.   Evaluate the climate of the Sunday School and of each class:

A. Do people know each other on a first-name basis?

B. Do people feel comfortable and relaxed in each other's presence? What changes might be needed to improve this?

C. Are new persons warmly introduced and accepted?

1. Do new persons and regular class members feel at home?
2. Is there a good balance between the introduction of persons and the simple acceptance of their being present without too much ado?
3. What changes are in order to help all persons feel welcomed and at home?

VI. Examine the content and teaching methods used in Sunday School classes. (Nothing discourages faithful Sunday School attendance like poorly planned and poorly conducted sessions.)

A. Are Sunday School class sessions carefully and prayerfully prepared?
B. List the various learning activities used in your class.
   - Discussion
   - Audiovisual presentation (DVD, VHS, PowerPoint, charts, etc.)
   - Lecture (teacher or student shares a lesson with the class members; usually one person provides the information)
   - Buzz groups (small discussion groups)
   - Role-play (role-playing a Bible character or assuming a role given by the teacher)
   - Panel presentations and discussions

C. List ways the Bible is used and studied in class sessions.
D. Brainstorm ideas that could improve Sunday School sessions and make them more interesting.

VII. Close with a time of prayer and dedication.

Method 10: Know and Understand Your Students

Purpose: To guide local church leaders in examining how well they know and understand the people currently in the class and those who could attend the Sunday School and other church activities

Setting: Teachers' Meeting

Session Outline:

I. Who are the people of our church and Sunday School?

A.   Post names of all persons and families on a wall.

Prior to the meeting, a small group should list on separate 5-by-8-inch cards (this will allow space for additional information about the families) every home represented in the church and each person living in the homes.

1.   Be sure to include not only families and individuals who attend regularly but also those who seldom or never attend and yet consider this congregation their home church.

2.   Be especially sensitive to those with special needs:
   •   disabled persons
   •   older persons
   •   singles
   •   single parents

B.   Study and discuss Mark 8:1–10. Focus on Jesus' sensitivity to the needs of the people and His response to their needs.

II.   What do we know about the people?

Add to each card information the church has about each family—places of employment, ages of children and grandchildren, special hobbies, interests, special needs and concerns, etc.

III. What do we need to know?

Attach to each card, or write on the cards, notes indicating additional information helpful to have for planning and deepening our fellowship.

1.   Significant experiences
2.   Home situations
3.   Community involvement
4.   Attitudes, feelings, motives
5.   Skills, understandings, and gifts
6.   Expectations and hopes

IV. How can we come to know each other more deeply?

A. On a chalkboard or newsprint, list all the things that might be done to develop deeper knowledge and understanding of each other in the church community. Here are a few ideas: interviews, name tags, visits in each other's homes, more small groups, written surveys, and opinion surveys.

B. Close the session by noting discoveries and implications for strengthening the church and Sunday School and by having a time of prayer.

Method 11: Find Quality Adult Sunday School Leaders and Teachers

This step will help the Sunday School superintendent, director of Christian education, or Christian education committee get to know their teachers and leaders by relating to them through interpersonal activities.

Take about 45–60 minutes to schedule some quality time with your teachers and leaders. This can be done with individuals or with a group of teachers and leaders of Christian education.

1. Make excellence your aim. Celebrate excellence. After all, skilled, committed leaders and teachers attract other potential leaders.

2. Keep a file or list of potential leaders. Record previous experience, special training, interests, and concerns.

3. Build a sense of family among leaders. A group of workers having fun together invites others to share in a serving, caring family.

4. Appoint a special leadership committee to study and list needs for present and potential leaders and to evaluate the effectiveness of present leaders.

5. Recognize and celebrate service being given. Highlight the exciting rewards of teaching. Too much good service goes unnoticed and uncelebrated, so celebrate the service given as much or more than the person giving it. The task is important as well as the person.

6. Take time for personal interviews with all persons now serving and with potential leaders as well. It may seem unnecessary, but it can provide surprising rewards. Talk with them about successes they have enjoyed, curriculum materials and usage, problems with students, and overall insights they have gained.

7. Know what your minimal standards and skill levels are for effective service and leadership.

8. Help all persons recognize their gifts and strengths. Develop these gifts and assist the workers in formal and informal ways.

9. Limit terms of service to one year at a time, or in some cases three or six months at a time. Few people want to sign up for life. Give sabbaticals for effective service.

10. Offer exploratory training opportunities. For those who are interested in teaching and leading but who are not yet ready to sign up, provide a time for consideration and to try out skills and interests.

Method 12: Celebrate the Sunday School through Special Events

There are many holidays that we celebrate nationally. Every local church will benefit its members and community by highlighting the important aspects of these special occasions. For example, Christmas can be a time for a special music concert, such as the Cantata; Thanksgiving can provide a service of worship with emphasis on being thankful to God for His bountiful blessings. To promote continued awareness and knowledge of African American achievements and contributions to society, Martin L. King Day should definitely be lifted up as well as Black History Month.

Special Days

- Rally Day—This is a Sunday in September chosen to emphasize the Sunday School, to dedicate teachers and workers, and to enroll children, youth, and adults in Sunday School. Start planning for this event in May or June so that it can be an exciting, well-run day.

- Harvest Day—On a Sunday in October or November, bring special offerings and gifts to thank God for the seasons of life. It can be a homecoming for persons who once attended Sunday School and worship but haven't done so recently or for those who have moved away but would welcome the opportunity to renew contact with friends and acquaintances.

- Christmas Sunday—Make this Sunday a time to celebrate God's love revealed in Jesus Christ. This is also a great time to help persons gain a new understanding of God's love by attending Sunday School and special class parties during the Christmas season.

- Easter Sunday—This is a traditional time for many to attend worship who do not usually come. It is also an opportune time to reach persons for the Sunday School.

- Mother's Day—Sunday School is for mothers and fathers also. Plan ways Sunday School classes can help parents and families on this special day.

- Martin Luther King Jr. Day—Dr. King's birthday, January 15th (celebrated the third Monday in January), is a time to celebrate his life and legacy.

- Black History Month—Throughout the month of February, celebrate the history and achievements of African Americans and people of color over the centuries.

Special Activities

- A church may want to offer family life seminars and other special activities as a Sunday School elective. Designate four or five Sundays for this purpose. Make a special effort to get persons and families of the community to enroll and attend.

- Select other ways to plan for increasing Sunday School attendance.

Special Emphases

- Focus on families. Families come in a variety of groupings, sizes, and ages.

- Focus on singles. Over 50 percent of all persons over 21 years of age in the United States are single. We have focuses on the family; now is the time to focus on singles. Involve single persons in the planning and implementation.

- Focus on retired persons. Retired persons are in a wide variety of age groups. Involve such persons in planning the focus.

- Focus on peace. World peace, and peace in our nation, are major concerns. Violence seems to be everywhere—on television, in movies, as well as in real life. There is no way to peace; peace *is* the way! Pull together a planning committee to help your congregation better work with God to bring peace on earth and reconciliation among individuals.

- Focus on faith. The Sunday School and the whole church are committed to helping everyone to grow in faith. Faith is a way of knowing and a way of living. Plan ways the church can build up and express faith more effectively.

Method 13: Strengthen and Support the Sunday School as a Pastor

Pastors are such influential figures in churches that their support for the Sunday

School is critical. Here are some guidelines for pastors to remember:

1. Believe in Christian education and the Sunday School.
2. Remain informed about Christian education and know what is happening in the Sunday School.
3. Know, visit, and support all Sunday School teachers and workers.
4. Teach an occasional short-term Sunday School unit in the children's, youth, and adult departments.
5. Greet persons on a first-name basis as they come to Sunday School.
6. Look for prospects for all Sunday School classes.
7. Participate in the Sunday School teacher enlistment process.
8. Support, participate, and lead in the fellowship and training sessions for Sunday School teachers and workers.
9. Know your Sunday School materials and encourage their use by teachers.
10. Encourage Sunday School teachers and workers to attend seminars, workshops, effective teaching labs, and other training events.
11. Support Christian education events in your state, area, or district.
12. Recognize the Sunday School in your sermons and encourage attendance.
13. Promote Christian education and the Sunday School in your church bulletin and newsletter.
14. Work closely with the Sunday School superintendent and other persons who carry responsibility for the work of the Sunday School.
15. Encourage the whole church to undergird the Sunday School with prayer and attendance.
16. Make clear to all adults that Sunday School is a growing experience for adults as well as children and youth.

Method 14: Consider Implementing These Sunday School Classes

The following class descriptions will stimulate thought about the classes that may be missing from your Sunday School program. The goal here is to bring awareness to leaders and teachers to consider and plan for those whose needs go unmet.

1. A class for adults with learning disabilities.
2. A class for high school youth who do not feel at home in regular adult classes.

3. A class especially for Sunday School dropouts of any age.

4. A class for those confined to nursing homes.

5. A class for young singles who have just started college or trade school or who are working at their first full-time job.

6. A class for young adults in their mid-20s to early 30s.

7. A class for parents who are having trouble dealing with adolescents.

8. A class for adults going through the changes and transitions of middle adulthood.

9. A class for older adults who want to make the last third of their lives especially significant.

10. An intergenerational class made up of teens, young adults, middle adults, and older adults. (Try it for a quarter.)

11. A class for doubters and questioners of any age. Allow in the class only those who are struggling and searching for a more meaningful faith.

12. A class for those recently separated, divorced, or widowed.

CHAPTER 16

ENERGIZING METHODS 15 THROUGH 17

Method 15: Ask Yourself, Am I an Exciting Teacher?

God already knows our strengths and weaknesses even though we are sometimes blind to them ourselves. Spend a few minutes filling out the evaluation below to gain a better understanding of your abilities to function as an effective teacher.

Place an "X" under the appropriate response beside each statement that reflects where you are now. The five rating choices are A=Always, O=Often, S=Sometimes, SL=Seldom, N=Never.

An exciting teacher is one who guides:	A	O	S	SL	N
1. I ask for the Holy Spirit's guidance as I guide learners.	—	—	—	—	—
2. I study the biblical truths and relate them to my own life before the session.	—	—	—	—	—
3. I pay attention to the individual growth needs of learners.	—	—	—	—	—
4. I formulate specific objectives for learners.	—	—	—	—	—
5. I plan for maximum student learning.	—	—	—	—	—
6. I create a learning atmosphere in the classroom.	—	—	—	—	—
7. I am excited when learners discover Bible truths for themselves.	—	—	—	—	—
8. I evaluate each learner's progress in and out of class.	—	—	—	—	—

An exciting teacher is one who guides:	A	O	S	SL	N
9. I guide learners by modeling for them a positive Christian example.	—	—	—	—	—
10. I arrive at the classroom ahead of students.	—	—	—	—	—
11. I am prepared to teach each session.	—	—	—	—	—
An exciting teacher is one who stimulates and motivates:					
12. I select learning activities that interest and challenge learners.	—	—	—	—	—
13. I allow learners plenty of room to explore and discover God's truth for themselves.	—	—	—	—	—
14. I encourage learners to be honest in expressing their ideas and feelings, even if they are wrong.	—	—	—	—	—
15. I assist learners in making plans for changing their behavior based on what they discover.	—	—	—	—	—
16. I encourage learners in spiritual decisions and/or behavior changes they make	—	—	—	—	—
An exciting teacher is one who models:					
17. I show learners how to love by loving them with a Christlike love.	—	—	—	—	—
18. I allow learners to explore my life as an example of a Christian both in and out of class.	—	—	—	—	—
19. I talk to students freely about my own adventures in following Christ (both successes and failures).	—	—	—	—	—
20. I model genuine concern for others.	—	—	—	—	—
21. I support the total program of the church.	—	—	—	—	—
An exciting teacher is one who cares:					
22. I know each learner as a person, not just as one of the students.	—	—	—	—	—

	A	O	S	SL	N
23. I accept each learner right where he or she is.	—	—	—	—	—
24. I show interest in each learner by listening carefully to what he or she has to say.	—	—	—	—	—
25. I actively affirm the personal worth of each learner.	—	—	—	—	—
26. I spend time praying for each learner by name.	—	—	—	—	—
27. I give time to each learner outside of class, as needed.	—	—	—	—	—
28. I am a real person and friend to each learner, not just a teacher.	—	—	—	—	—
29. I care for learners by maintaining discipline in the classroom.	—	—	—	—	—
30. I check up on absentees to show them that I missed them.	—	—	—	—	—
31. I care for learners by evaluating my teaching effectiveness.	—	—	—	—	—
32. I care for learners by improving my teaching skills.	—	—	—	—	—

Provide written responses to the open-ended questions below.

33. What have I discovered from this evaluation? _____

_____

34. What steps am I going to take to improve my teaching and leadership?_____

_____

_____

35. How will this self-evaluation help me in my teaching?_____

_____

Method 16: Job Description to Evaluate the Sunday School Superintendent

If you are a Sunday School superintendent, this form will expose you to a variety of duties and responsibilities that apply to your role as superintendent. No one person can expect to do all of the things mentioned here, however, the job description should bring about a heightened awareness of what is expected of a Sunday School superintendent.

A. As an *organizer*, the Sunday School superintendent is to...

1. Be responsible for the total activities of the children's, youth, and adult divisions.
2. Supervise and coordinate the activities of all teachers, workers, division coordinators, and officers of the Sunday School.
3. Develop, with the board of Christian education, a guiding philosophy for the Sunday School, with written objectives.
4. Provide a graded program of instruction.
5. Provide job descriptions for all teachers and officers of the Sunday School.

B. As an *administrator*, the Sunday School superintendent is to...

6. Work with the pastor, board of Christian education, and minister of Christian education in planning the entire program.
7. Help to coordinate the activities of various groups and departments.
8. Serve as a member of the board of Christian education.
9. Hold quarterly conferences with officers and teachers.
10. Make a periodic inspection of Christian education equipment and classrooms, offering recommendations to the property board.
11. Supervise the Christian education budget.
12. Direct workers' conferences.
13. Maintain a master calendar of the year's programs and activities.
14. Help to determine policies involving the enrollment and assignment of pupils and plan for annual promotions.
15. Make a periodic report to the board of Christian education and the congregation.
16. Keep up with trends and new ideas by reading books and magazines on Christian education and attending conferences and conventions.
17. Help to nominate department leaders, teachers, and other workers.
18. Help to make decisions concerning curriculum materials and supplies.

19. Supervise the keeping of records and utilize them for improvements.

20. Help to establish an absentee follow-up system.

21. Constantly study the use of space and the grading system.

22. Stress the importance of evangelism and mission in all classes.

23. Begin and end the Sunday School on time.

C. As a *supervisor*, the Sunday School superintendent is to…

24. Observe each class in action at least once per year.

25. Constantly stress the need for quality and improvement.

26. Direct the evaluation and measurement of progress and achievement.

27. Help to establish objectives for the entire program.

28. Help each department to define its objectives.

29. Make available materials and tools for teaching and working.

30. Serve as a counselor to all teachers and workers.

31. Provide assistance in solving problems in teaching and learning.

32. Work with the pastor and/or minister of Christian education in setting up and maintaining a program of teacher training.

33. Keep a record of all curriculum materials being used.

D. The Sunday School superintendent's *pre-session duties* are to

34. Be present 30 minutes prior to Sunday School to make sure everything is in order for the school to begin.

35. Use the pre-session time for checking on staff and equipment.

E. The Sunday School superintendent's *Sunday duties* are to …

36. Help greet people.

37. Assist new people in getting to their classes.

38. See that literature is distributed.

39. Keep alert for needs and achievements of the classes and departments.

40. Give an attendance report to the pastor.

41. Write an interesting article for the church paper promoting the Sunday School.

F. The Sunday School superintendent's *weekly duties* are to . . .

42. Direct promotional activities.
43. Keep the records up-to-date.
44. Train prospective teachers.
45. Recruit substitutes when needed.
46. Keep one lesson for each class on file for a substitute to use if needed.
47. Publicly express appreciation for the work of teachers and workers.
48. Help teachers to follow up with pupils.
49. Visit other Sunday Schools when possible and take along a teacher.

G. The Sunday School superintendent's *monthly duties* are to . . .

50. Attend the meetings of the board of Christian education.
51. Direct workers' conferences.
52. Monitor attendance trends.
53. Review and set standards for the Sunday School.
54. Order new curriculum materials at least six weeks prior to needing them.

H. The Sunday School superintendent's *annual duties* are to . . .

55. Make an annual evaluation and submit a report to the pastor for the annual church report.
56. Plan the Sunday School budget with the board of Christian education.
57. Submit a report regarding audiovisual needs. (Try to add at least one piece of new equipment each year.)
58. Attend at least one convention and one workshop.
59. Help to plan an appreciation banquet for teachers.
60. Help to plan the annual Christian education budget.
61. Guide staff in setting enrollment and attendance growth goals.
62. Help to establish annual objectives based on needs.

63. Constantly seek to inspire and motivate workers.

64. Continually look for potential teachers to train for the future.

65. Guide the Sunday School staff in planning two major growth campaigns—one in the fall and one in the spring.

Method 17: Conduct an Overview of Your Sunday School Program

Evaluate each of the following areas by marking the appropriate box.

G = Good, OK = Okay, NH = Needs Help

1. Curriculum Selection and Usage	G	OK	NH
a. Are all board members and Sunday School teachers aware of and trained in the use of the church's Bible-based materials?	—	—	—
b. Who decides what materials will be used?	—	—	—
c. How are teachers prepared for using curriculum materials?	—	—	—
d. How are curriculum materials reviewed and evaluated?	—	—	—
e. How is the use of curriculum materials reviewed and evaluated?	—	—	—
f. What criteria are used for evaluating curriculum?	—	—	—
2. Teacher and Leader Enlistment, Support, and Encouragement			
a. Who decides who will be asked to teach?	—	—	—
b. Who decides who will teach where?	—	—	—
c. By whom and how are teachers evaluated?	—	—	—
d. How are teachers recruited and terminated?	—	—	—
e. What is the length of term teachers are asked to serve?	—	—	—
f. How is appreciation shown to teachers?	—	—	—
g. How are teachers supported and encouraged throughout the year?	—	—	—

	G	OK	NH
h. Who is responsible for honoring teachers?	—	—	—
i. What minimal teaching skills are persons expected to have?	—	—	—
j. Who reviews the skills of teachers and determines the kinds of skill training to be planned?	—	—	—
k. Who plans enrichment and refreshment experiences for persons now teaching?	—	—	—
l. How is teacher effectiveness evaluated?	—	—	—
3. *Creative Use of the Physical Plant*			
a. How fresh and up-to-date are the classrooms?	—	—	—
b. Who is responsible for keeping the rooms clean and fresh?	—	—	—
c. Who determines the standards for freshness and neatness of classrooms?	—	—	—
d. Who decides which classes use which rooms?	—	—	—
4. *Number Enrolled in the Sunday School and Percentage Attending Each Sunday*			
a. Who is responsible for maintaining enrollment numbers and attendance percentages?	—	—	—
b. How well is the congregation informed about enrollment and attendance trends?	—	—	—
c. What criteria are used for adding or deleting names from Sunday School enrollment?	—	—	—
d. Who determines such criteria?	—	—	—
5. *Proportion of Those Attending Morning Worship Who Also Attend Sunday School*			
a. Who is responsible for comparing morning worship with Sunday School enrollments and attendees?	—	—	—
b. What efforts are made to encourage persons attending morning worship to attend Sunday School and vice versa, and who is responsible for doing this?	—	—	—

	G	OK	NH
6. *Evidence of Long-Range Planning and Goal Setting for Christian Education and the Sunday School*			
a. Who is responsible for long-range planning?	—	—	—
b. When is long-range planning usually done, and when was it last done?	—	—	—
c. How is the whole church involved in long-range planning?	—	—	—
d. How are long-range planning and progress toward goals reported to the entire church?	—	—	—
e. What current long-term goals are guiding the work of the Sunday School?	—	—	—
7. *Image of the Sunday School in the Life of the Church*			
a. How important is the Sunday School to the church's total life and ministry?	—	—	—
b. How is the importance of the Sunday School measured and discussed?	—	—	—
c. What words are used by the pastor, key leaders, and members of the church when talking about the Sunday School?	—	—	—
8. *Percentage of the Total Church Budget Devoted to Christian Education and the Sunday School*			
a. Who determines how much of the budget goes to the work of the Sunday School?	—	—	—
b. What criteria are used to determine budget needs of the Sunday School?	—	—	—
c. What portion of the Christian education and Sunday School budget must be financed outside the total church budget?	—	—	—
9. *Availability of Resources in Addition to Curriculum Materials for the Teaching Ministry of the Sunday School*			
a. Is a resource library of audiovisuals, art supplies, and study resources maintained by the church for its teachers?	—	—	—

	G	OK	NH
b. Who is responsible for planning and maintaining a teachers' resource library?	—	—	—
10. *Outreach to Visitors, Prospects, Absentees, and Regular Attendees*			
a. Are visitors' names and addresses recorded and filed?	—	—	—
b. Are visitors contacted within a week of their visit?	—	—	—
c. Who is responsible for contacting visitors?	—	—	—
d. Who is responsible for contacting absentees?	—	—	—
e. Who determines when absentees should be contacted?	—	—	—
f. Are the reasons for absences periodically explored and examined?	—	—	—
g. Are class members encouraged to invite friends and relatives to attend Sunday School?	—	—	—
h. Is there a system for inviting persons to enroll in Sunday School? Who is responsible for enrolling new persons?	—	—	—
i. Are inactive members and attendees contacted periodically?	—	—	—
11. *Record System that Enables the Sunday School Staff and the Whole Church to Stay in Touch with and Care for Individual Persons*			
a. What system is now used? Is it adequate? What changes are needed?	—	—	—
b. Does the record system provide a sound basis for visitation and absentee follow-up?	—	—	—
12. *Programs, Sunday Sessions, and Ministries of the Sunday School Match the Expectations and Needs of Children, Youth, and Adults*			
a. How are the expectations and needs of children, youth, and adults known and assessed?	—	—	—

	G	OK	NH
b. Who is responsible for the assessing and the matching?	—	—	—
c. What feedback system is used to get such information? Who is responsible for designing and using the feedback system?	—	—	—

The role that Sunday School plays in the life of the local church should never be underestimated in terms of its importance. The activities and evaluations listed in this chapter will help to strengthen teachers, superintendents, administrators, and ultimately, the congregation.

APPENDIX

RESOURCES FOR THOSE
WHO TEACH, LEARN, AND LEAD IN
ADULT CHRISTIAN EDUCATION

Study Bibles

Daily Study Bible for Men. Wheaton, IL: Tyndale Publishing House, 1999. Essays and Bible study geared for men.

Hebrew-Greek Study Bible. Iowa City, IA: World Bible Publishers, 1988. Has Strong's dictionary and vocabulary help. Red-letter edition.

Life Application Bible (NIV). Wheaton, IL: Tyndale Publishing House, 1991. A good Bible for teachers, ministers, and those who desire personal growth and enrichment with real-life applications.

Life Recovery Bible (LB). Wheaton, IL: Tyndale Publishing House, 1992. In this edition, the popular *Living Bible* takes on new meaning for Christian educators who are looking for a Bible to reach persons addicted to alcohol and other drugs. The notes and helps are based on the 12-step recovery program, with many helpful Bible passages to give support to the earnest seeker.

Men of Color Bible (KJV). Atlanta: Nia Publishing, 2002. Many helpful notes and articles for and about men of African descent.

The New Analytical Bible and Dictionary (KJV). Chicago: John A. Dickson Publishing, 1980. This Bible has four workbooks with topical study notes, outlines of each book, and much more.

The New Oxford Annotated Bible with the Apocrypha (RSV). New York: Oxford University Press, 1991. Good exegetical notes and introduction to each book of the Bible. Added features of this Bible are the Apocryphal books, which have been excluded from most of the major Protestant translations.

The NIV Study Bible (NIV). Grand Rapids, MI: Zondervan Publishing House, 1985. Includes a clear introduction to each book of the Bible, with many excellent historical and archaeological study notes.

Original African Heritage Bible (KJV). Nashville: James C. Winston Publishing, 1993. Persons who desire to know about Black people in the Bible will find this Bible valuable.

The Thompson Chain-Reference Bible. Indianapolis: B. B. Kirkbride Bible Co., 1980. This is a user-friendly Bible with all the helps one will need to do in-depth Bible study.

The Wesley Bible. Nashville: Thomas Nelson Publishers, 1990. A personal study Bible with a Wesleyan theological perspective.

Bible Translations

The Amplified Bible. Grand Rapids, MI: Zondervan Publishing House, 1987.

Eight Translations of the New Testament. Wheaton, IL: Tyndale Publishing House, 1974. Includes King James, Living Bible, Phillips Modern English, Revised Standard Version, Today's English Version, New International Version, Jerusalem Bible, and New English Version.

The Word: The Bible from 26 Translations. Moss Point, MS: Mathis Publishers, 1988. Good when looking for a new translation or insight from the Bible.

Word Study Books and Concordances

Barclay, William. *New Testament Words.* Philadelphia: Westminster Press, 1974. Many New Testament words with Greek background. A companion to *Barclay's Daily Bible Study.*

Falwell, Jerry. *Parallel Bible Commentary* (KJV). Nashville: Thomas Nelson Publishers, 1994. A Bible comprehensive in scope, with many useful helps for the busy Sunday School teacher or pastor. Contains outlines, maps, word explanations, and much more.

Strong, James. *Strong's Concordance.* Nashville: Abingdon Press, 1977. Originally published in 1890, this is still one of the most-utilized reference books on Old and New Testament words. Keyed to the King James Version. A good reference for the lay teacher.

Vine, W. E. *Old and New Testaments Exposition Dictionary.* Old Tappan, NJ: Fleming H. Revell Co., 1970. Helps students who don't know biblical Hebrew or

Greek to understand the language of the Bible.

Walvoord, John F., *Bible Knowledge Commentary*, ed. 2 vols. Elgin, IL: Cook Communications, 1980. These volumes are full of study aids to help you grasp the meaning of the biblical text, including book outlines, cross references, maps, charts, and Old and New Testament commentary.

Whitaker, Richard E., and James E. Goehring, *The Eerdmans Analytical Concordance to the Revised Standard Version*. Grand Rapids, MI: Wm. B. Eerdmans Publishing Co., 1998. A resource for Bible students to the RSV. Superb scholarship and easy to handle for those who are not literate in biblical languages.

Zodhiates, Spiros, ed. *The Complete Word Study of the New Testament* (KJV). Chattanooga, TN: AMG Publishers, 1992. Written in Greek and English and suitable for use in studying the Greek language. This is one of the best books for persons who want to get closer to the original Greek language.

Christian Education: Adult and Family Life

Fowler, James W. *Stages of Faith*. San Francisco: Harper, 1981. Fowler's definition of faith is both secular and religious. His research includes in-depth interviews and conversations with a wide range of individuals who share their stories of meaning and faith.

Gangel, Kenneth O., and Warren S. Benson. *Christian Education: Its History and Philosophy*. Chicago: Moody Press, 1983. A survey, beginning with biblical times and working upward to the present-day history of Christian education. Fails to mention the role of African Americans in the struggle of the Sunday School and the Christian education movement.

———. *The Christian Educator's Handbook on Family Life Education*. Grand Rapids: Baker Books, 1996. Spells out a number of critical issues facing the family.

Gangel, Kenneth O., and Howard G. Hendricks. *The Christian Educator's Handbook on Teaching*. Grand Rapids, MI: Baker Books, 1988. This is a complete resource on Christian education and teaching. Useful for the home, church, and school.

Gangel, Kenneth O., and James C. Wilhoit, eds. *The Christian Educator's Handbook on Adult Education*. Grand Rapids, MI: Baker Books, 1997. A compilation of many helpful articles dealing with the theory and practice of Christian adult education.

Kennedy, Carroll E. *Human Development: The Adult Years and Aging.* New York: Macmillan, 1978. One of the best books on adult development, this volume examines the successive stages of young, middle, and older adults. The writing style is easy to understand by the average layperson.

Knowles, Malcolm S. *The Modem Practice of Adult Education.* New York: Association Press, 1970. This is still one of the best books on adult learners. Knowles points out in vivid detail the distinctions between andragogy (adult learner) and pedagogy (child learner). A text and guide for students, teachers of adults, and planners of adult education.

Levinson, Daniel J., et al. *The Seasons of a Man's Life.* New York: Ballantine, 1978. Explores and explains the specific periods of personal development through which humans pass and the common patterns underlying the human condition.

McIntosh, Gary L. *One Church, Four Generations.* Grand Rapids, MI: Baker Books, 2004. This is must reading for anyone who wishes to understand how each present-day generation differs from the others. McIntosh provides thoughtful insight into the values, qualities, and social trends that have shaped the four generations. This book gives the best description of Builders, Boomers, Busters, and Bridgers (Millennials).

Peterson, Gilbert A., ed. *The Christian Education of Adults.* Chicago: Moody Press, 1984. Dr. Peterson has compiled some of the most creative methods, techniques, and approaches to adult education in the local church. This book can strengthen the Christian education of adults in most local congregations.

Powers, Bruce P. *Christian Education Handbook.* Nashville: Broadman Press, 1981. A book for directors of Christian education, pastors, and planners of Christian education for local, state, and national programs.

Reed, James, and Ronnie Prevost. *A History of Christian Education.* Nashville: Broadman & Holman, 1998. This is a textbook written for Christian education courses. It is also a good reference tool for directors of Christian education who wish to enrich their knowledge about our Christian heritage.

Seymour, Jack, et al. *Contemporary Approaches to Christian Education.* Nashville: Abingdon Press, 1982. The writers of this book examine five approaches by which contemporary Christian educators can develop their theory and practice in religious instruction. These approaches include faith community development, liberation, and interpretation.

————. *Educating Christians.* Nashville: Abingdon Press, 1993. This book begins with the premise that to minister to people inside or outside the church we need to understand their needs and, more particularly, understand how to help individuals make meaning out of their life experiences. Topics the authors explore include the meaning of faith, educating toward vocation, Christian education for teaching, and justice.

Spindle, Richard. *A Breath of Fresh Air: Christian Education of Adults in the 21st Century.* Kansas City, MO: Beacon Hill Press, 2000. Dr. Spindle discusses what adults want and need in their Sunday School classes. He also points to some of the social and cultural obstacles that have emerged in Christian education, and he considers the theological and biblical descriptions of what adult education is.

Stokes, Kenneth, ed. *Faith Development in the Adult Life Cycle.* Chicago: W. H. Sadlier, Inc., 1982. This book records the 1981 Faith Development Symposium research papers from many well-known scholars, including Malcolm Knowles, Winston Gooden, James Fowler, Mary Wilcox, and Linda J. Vogel.

Stubblefield, Jerry M. *A Church Ministering to Adults.* Nashville: Broadman Press, 1986. This book is designed to be a comprehensive resource on how a congregation can minister to the adult learner. The topics include adult Christian education, program planning, and adult development.

Vogel, Linda J. *The Religious Education of Older Adults.* Birmingham, AL: Religious Education Press, 1984. A book designed to help the Christian educator understand some of the social, spiritual, psychological, and educational needs of older adults.

Westerhoff, John H. *Will Our Children Have Faith?* New York: Seabury, 1976. Westerhoff makes a bold declaration proposing an end to the Schooling Instructional method in which schooling is the method and teaching-learning is the means. He proposes that the curriculum for the church ought to be an interactive process that takes place within the community of faith.

Zuck, Roy B. *Adult Education in the Church.* Chicago: Moody Press, 1970. Some of the topics covered are the learning process of adults, methods for teaching adults, family life, and sex education. The writer deals with the *how*, rather than with theories, of Christian adult education.

Teaching and Spiritual Growth

Blair, Christine E. *The Art of Teaching the Bible: A Practical Guide for Adults.* Louisville, KY: Geneva Press, 2001. Based on sound principles of teaching adults, this book includes chapters on the five "R's": 1) Remembering what they have learned; 2) Revisiting the biblical text; 3) Reflecting critically about what they have learned; 4) Reinterpreting in an analytical and imaginative way; and 5) Responding by discovering possible actions to be taken to implement the biblical text.

Bridges, Jerry. *True Fellowship: The Biblical Practice of Koinonia.* Colorado Springs, CO: NavPress, 1985. A well-written exposition on the meaning of Christian fellowship. Beginning with fellowship with God, it moves to the broader meaning of *koinonia* within the body of Christ.

Bruce, Barbara. *7 Ways of Teaching the Bible to Adults.* Nashville: Abingdon Press, 2000. By incorporating the research of Howard Gardner of Harvard University concerning the seven intelligences from his brain research on adults, Bruce devotes seven brief chapters on how to optimize the learning of adult students.

———. *Start Here: Teaching and Learning with Adults.* Nashville: Abingdon Press, 1999. Practical ideas and teaching techniques to help teachers plan and inspire their students to learn.

Culley, Iris V. *Education for Spiritual Growth.* San Francisco: Harper & Row, 1984. Here the reader will discover a number of ways to cultivate the inner life. The author discusses Christian and non-Christian paths to spiritual growth.

Halverson, Delia. *Leading Adult Learners.* Nashville: Abingdon Press, 1995. *Leading Adult Learners* is a resource for teachers, class leaders, Christian educators, and members of adult Sunday School classes, with guidance for starting a new class.

Hull, John M. *What Prevents Adults from Learning.* Philadelphia: Trinity Press, 1991. This book outlines the challenges that the modern world offers to the adult learner. In a religious context, Hull also explores the deep-seated need to be right, the pain of learning, and the conflict of change.

Iris, Marie. *Fashion Me a People: Curriculum in the Church.* Louisville, KY: Westminster John Knox Press, 1989. This is a book that should be on the shelf of every Christian educator. Part two of the book outlines the nature of the church's curriculum and calling by putting forth the following educational forms: *koinonia* (community), *leiturgia* (prayer), *didache* (teaching), *kerygma* (proclamation), and *diakonia* (service).

Juengst, Sara Covin. *Equipping the Saints.* Louisville, KY: Westminster John Knox Press, 1998. This book attempts to address the challenge of how to prepare those who feel the call to teach. The book covers a nine-month teacher training course that includes Bible background, basic Christian beliefs, and sound teaching techniques.

Leypoldt, Martha. *40 Ways to Teach in Groups*. Valley Forge, PA: Judson Press, 1967. Although this book is nearly four decades old, it is still one of the best books on teaching adults or children and youth. Each method that is presented is illustrated with how-to approaches.

———. *Learning Is Change: Adult Education in the Church*. Valley Forge, PA: Judson Press, 1971. The aim of this book is to enable the teacher and student to change their attitudes, the way they learn about their faith, and their actions. Should be required reading for every teacher, pastor, and Christian educator.

Vos, Howard F. *Effective Bible Study*. Grand Rapids, MI: Zondervan Publishing House, 1973. The author provides 16 ways to present a lesson to students. It is rich in biblical content and sound in methodology.

Warren, Rick. *Dynamic Bible Study*. Wheaton, IL: Victor Books, 1989. This book has been used as a standard text for Bible colleges and seminaries. The teaching methods presented are some of the best I have read and taught.

Willmington, H. L. *The Complete Bible Lists*. Wheaton, IL: Tyndale Publishing House, 1987. A curious collection of unusual statistics from the Bible. With this information at your disposal, you will never have a dull moment in your class.

Biblical and Social Values

Collins, Marva. *Values: Lighting the Candles of Excellence*. Los Angeles: Dove Books, 1996. Marva Collins has written a book that will help children and youth if the values she has listed are adhered to. This is more than a book of essays; this is a moral guide for living. She writes about 26 values in alphabetical style. If you are a parent or grandparent, get a copy for your child.

Malphurs, Aubrey. *Values-Driven Leadership*. Grand Rapids, MI: Baker Books, 1999. A work that will help individuals and congregations to define and develop their core values.

Pilch, John J., and J. Malina. *Handbook of Biblical Social Values*. Peabody, MA: Hendrickson Publishers, 1998. Over 100 entries explain the values in Bible times. Some of the topics covered are freedom, obedience, family, power, love, sin, and justice.

Wright, Carl Jeffery. *God's Vision or Television?* Chicago: Urban Ministries, Inc., 2004. This long-awaited book is packed with useful information on how television influences and manipulates our minds, manners, and overall behaviors. The book is biblically based and offers a scriptural alternative to the lies and vision that television portrays in contrast to what God says.

Christian Education in the African American Tradition

Carter, Harold A. *The Prayer Tradition of Black People.* Valley Forge, PA: Judson Press, 1976. Dr. Carter has rendered a valuable service in the creation of this book by reminding all Black Christians of how important prayer is for spiritual growth as well as social progress. Prayer, says Carter, is a great reservoir of faith and culture.

Chism, Keith A. *Christian Education for the African-American Community.* Nashville: Discipleship Resources, 1995. I found this book to be a good general reference on the teacher and the learner, but it lacks a strong emphasis on the Black experience in Christian education in general and the Sunday School in particular.

Crockett, Joseph V. *Teaching Scripture from an African-American Perspective.* Nashville: Discipleship Resources, 1991. I highly endorse this book because it is packed with wisdom and good content about Christian education in the African American church. Crockett draws on four teaching strategies: story, exile, sanctuary, and exodus. Each strategy highlights different dimensions in the African American experience.

Harris, James H. *Pastoral Theology: A Black Church Perspective.* Minneapolis: Fortress Press, 1991. Harris deals handily with a perspective on pastoral theology in the Black church. I found his chapter on Christian education to be on target. It is his position that Christian education in the African American church should have as its goal the liberation of Black people.

Ogbonnaya, A. Okehukwu. *African Ways: A Christian Education Philosophy.* Calumet City, IL: Urban Ministries, Inc., 2000. A scholarly book drawn from an African perspective. Its philosophical underpinnings carry a strong Afro-centric point of view that is rooted in a communal conceptual framework.

Paris, Peter J. *The Social Teaching of Black People.* Philadelphia: Fortress Press, 1985. The author gives a critical interpretation of moral and political values in the African American churches. Paris has a broad view that goes beyond Black liberation to what he calls Black tradition, which is a biblical vision that sees all humankind under the Fatherhood of God and the kinship of all peoples.

Wilkerson, Barbara. *Multicultural Religious Education*. Birmingham, AL: Religious Education Press, 1997. A book whose time has come and whose message should be welcomed by all. Multiculturalism is a statement about who God is and how this entire planet is related to Him. A well-written book on racial and ethnic diversity.

Wimberly, Anne S. *Soul Stories: African American Christian Education*. Nashville: Abingdon Press, 1994. The story-linking method is the process that Wimberly has adopted to educate African Americans. By reclaiming the story, we are able to get in touch with our roots and the meaning of life.

Afro-centric History

Anyike, James C. *African-American Holidays*. Chicago: Popular Truth, 1991. A guide to help Black Americans celebrate historical, religious, and cultural holidays.

Asante, Molefi Kere. *The Afro-centric Idea*. Philadelphia: Temple University Press, 1927. A well-written scholarly work with a focus on explaining the African ethos from an African worldview rather than a Euro-centric one. Asante moves beyond mere rhetoric to a more substantive view of ourselves as African people.

Copher, Charles B. *Black Biblical Studies*. Chicago: Black Light Fellowship, 1993. An anthology of the writings of Dr. Copher on Black people in the Bible.

Felder, Cain Hope. *Stony the Road We Trod*. Minneapolis: Fortress Press, 1991. Taking issue with those scholars who have ignored the Black presence in the Bible, 11 Black Bible scholars have redefined biblical authority and how the Bible is to be interpreted in light of new research about people of color in biblical times.

McCray, Walter. *The Black Presence in the Bible*, 2 vols. Chicago: Black Light Fellowship, 1991. Tracing our Black roots from the Table of Nations in Genesis 10, McCray has revealed the Hamitic genealogy and the long line of kings, queens, and nations in Scripture.

Ogbonnaya, A. Okechukwu. *Upon This Rock: African Influence in the Christian Church*. Calumet City, IL: Urban Ministries, Inc., 1999. This adult study of Africans in the Old and New Testaments and beyond provides a moving account of people of color in various geographical and social settings. This small booklet is packed with information about African people and the contributions they have made.

Snowden, Frank M. *Blacks in Antiquity*. London: Belknap Press, 1970. Dr. Snowden has assembled an impressive array of evidence from art, pottery, frescos, statues, and other artifacts supporting the fact that Black people were a part of Greek and Roman civilizations.

Wright, Jeremiah. *Africans Who Shaped Our Faith*. Calumet City, IL: Urban Ministries, Inc., 1995. This book contains 12 historical sermons about Black people found in the Bible. Dr. Wright raises many questions and answers them in his keen perception about the people he identifies as African Jews.

Books on the Black Family

Abatso, George, and Yvonne Abatso. *How to Equip the African-American Family*. Calumet City, IL: Urban Ministries, Inc., 1991. Each chapter contains case studies and Bible applications. A study guide prepared by Dr. Colleen Birchett makes the book more valuable for the teacher or Christian educator.

Billingsley, Andrew. *Climbing Jacob's Ladder*. New York: Simon & Schuster, 1992. One of the best books on the Black family. It covers the historical and social development of the Black family and incorporates the role of the Black church in shaping and impacting the family toward a positive pursuit. The book dispels misconceptions, misunderstandings, and misinformation about the Black family.

Blassingame, John W. *The Slave Community*. New York: Oxford University Press, 1972. Based on a rich variety of sources, both traditional and new, Blassingame has carefully described and analyzed the slave culture and its forms. He also points out how the cultural forms and the system of slavery affected Black people in America.

Matson, T. B. *The Bible and Family Relations*. Nashville: Broadman Press, 1983. This book covers every facet of the family to be found in the Bible. A herculean task to have written, and well worth the effort to read.

McAdoo, Harriette P., ed. *Black Families*. Beverly Hills, CA: Sage Publications, 1981. Harriette McAdoo has brought together many outstanding scholars, many of whom are noted Black researchers in the fields of sociology, psychology, and social work.

Smith, Leon. *Family Ministry: An Educational Resource for the Local Church*. Nashville: Discipleship Resources, 1975. This book is old, but if you can get your hands on a copy, do so. This book can help Christian educators and Sunday School boards make solid plans and implement effective family programs and ministries.

Smith, Wallace C. *The Church in the Life of the Black Family*. Valley Forge, PA: Judson Press, 1985. In this work, Smith has put his finger on the pulse of the Black family and those factors that have influenced their behavioral patterns. Wallace shows how resources can and ought to be designed for the education of families in the Black church.

Walker, Clarence. *Biblical Counseling with African-Americans*. Grand Rapids, MI: Zondervan Publishing House, 1992. Dr. Walker takes some of the principles of counseling and applies them to the story of the Ethiopian in Acts 8. He deals with ethnicity, gender, sexual power, socioeconomic, environmental, and religious issues. In part he shows how the counseling model can be used to help families, couples, and individuals.

Wimberly, Edward P. *Pastoral Counseling and Spiritual Values*. Nashville: Abingdon Press, 1982. Dr. Wimberly writes with insight and understanding about pastoral care for the Black family. He covers the theoretical and practical approaches to counseling and pastoral care in addition to prescribing sensible solutions to assist the Black family.

———. *Using Scripture in Pastoral Counseling*. Nashville: Abingdon Press, 1994. A widely respected leader in the pastoral counseling field, Dr. Wimberly has developed a model of pastoral care that combines a theoretical framework and utilizes Scripture and theories of counseling.

Singles Ministry

Koons, Carolyn A., and Michael J. Anthony. *Single Adult Passages*. Grand Rapids, MI: Baker Books, 1991. An in-depth study of Christian singles in America. The book offers a new awareness of their needs and some of the ways the Christian church can minister to those needs.

Leadership Development

Armerding, Hudson T. *The Heart of Godly Leadership*. Wheaton, IL: Crossway Books, 1992. The author shares some of the principles of biblical leadership and the importance of being an example to others. He draws on the examples of characters found in the Bible to illustrate his message.

Callahan, Kennon L. *Effective Church Leadership: Building on the Twelve Keys.* San Francisco: Harper & Row, 1990. This book offers a step-by-step approach to planning and leadership development. A good resource for pastors and planners of Christian education programs.

Goodwin, Bennie. *The Effective Leader.* Atlanta: Goodpatrick Publishers, 1995. Here is a book that clearly defines what Christian leadership is about and what Christian leaders are called to do. According to Dr. Goodwin, every Christian has a calling and a ministry to perform. However, one must be committed to growth and development to advance one's God-given ministry.

————. *Preparing God's People for Ministry.* Memphis: Church of God in Christ, 1994. Here is a little book that concisely details how God calls Christians to do ministry in the church and the world. This book introduces the reader to such topics as the meaning of Christian ministry, how to be effective as a leader, and how to minister in the African American church and community. In addition to outlining the risks and rewards of ministry, this book will help pastors and laypersons to lead God's people more effectively.

NOTES

Chapter 1

1. Joseph V. Crockett, *Teaching Scripture from an African-American Perspective* (Nashville: Discipleship Resources, 1991), p. 57.

2. Ibid., p. xii.

3. Charles Copher, *Black Biblical Studies: An Anthology of Charles Copher* (Chicago: Black Light Fellowship, 1993), p. 35.

4. Ibid.

5. Walter McCray, *The Black Presence in the Bible* (Chicago: Black Light Fellowship, 1991), p. 30.

6. Cain Hope Felder, *Troubling Biblical Waters* (New York: Orbis Books, 1990), p. 12.

7. Anthony Browder, *From the Browder File: 22 Essays on the African American Experience* (Washington, DC: Institute of Karmic Guidance, 1989), p. 19.

8. Edward Taylor, *Primitive Culture*, vol. 1 (New York: Harper & Row, 1958), p. 1.

Chapter 2

1. C. Eric Lincoln and Lawrence H. Mamiya, *The Black Church in the African American Experience* (Durham, NC: Duke University Press, 1990), pp. 251–2.

2. Peter Paris, *The Social Teaching of Black Churches* (Philadelphia: Fortress Press, 1985), pp. 67–68. This information was originally published in the *Journal of the 20th Quadrennial Session of the General Conference of the AME Church*, May 4, 1896, pp. 98–99.

3. James H. Harris, *Pastoral Theology: A Black Church Perspective* (Philadelphia: Fortress Press, 1991), pp. 104–5.

Part II

1.   Gary McIntosh, *One Church, Four Generations* (Grand Rapids, MI: Baker Books, 2004), pp. 27–42, 72–73, 122–125.

Chapter 3

1.   R. J. Havighurst, *Human Development and Education* (Chicago: University of Chicago Press, 1953), p. 16.

Chapter 4

1.   Carroll E. Kennedy, *Human Development: The Adult Years and Aging* (New York: Macmillan, 1978), p. 243.

2.   James W. Fowler, *Stages of Faith* (San Francisco: HarperCollins, 1995), pp. 151–99.

3.   John Westerhoff, *Will Our Children Have Faith?* (New York: Seabury, 1976), p. 89.

4. R. J. Havighurst, *Human Development and Education* (Chicago: University of Chicago Press, 1953), pp. 257–80.

Chapter 5

1.   "U.S. Bureau of Census Population of the U.S. by Age, Race, Hispanic Origin: 1993–2050," August 2003, pp. 1–6.

2.   Ibid., p. 3.

3.   Z. S. Blau, *Old Age in a Changing Society* (New York: Franklin Watts, 1973), pp. 2–3.

4.   *65+ in the United States: 2005, Current, Population Reports, Special Studies,* U.S. Department of Human Services, 2005. Pp 1–4; 5–7.

Chapter 6

1.   Kenneth Stokes, ed. *Faith Development in the Adult Life Cycle.* Malcolm Knowles, contributor. (New York: William Sadlier, 1983), pp. 63–64.

2.   Quoted in C. Edward Smith paper, "Trends in Christian Education" (Colorado Springs, CO: David C. Cook Publishing Co., 1984), p. 3.

3.   Harold A. Carter, *The Prayer Tradition of the Black Church* (Valley Forge, PA: Judson Press, 1976), p. 20.

4. E. M. Bounds, *Power through Prayer* (Grand Rapids, MI: Zondervan Publishing House, 1965), p. 12.

5. *Koinonia* is a Greek word, not an English one, so this is a transliteration rather than a translation.

6. "The Church Has One Foundation," *Hymnal of the Church of God* (Anderson, IN: Warner Press, 1989), no. 286.

7. Jerry Bridges, *True Fellowship* (Colorado Springs, CO: NavPress, 1985), pp. 54–55.

Chapter 7

1. Charles Shumate and Sherrill Hayes, eds., *Discover Your Gifts* (Anderson, IN: Board of Christian Education, 1990), p. 8.

2. Benjamin F. Reid, *Glory to the Spirit* (Los Angeles: First Church of God, 1990), p. 73.

3. Ibid., p. 32.

4. "O Church of God," *Hymnal of the Church of God* (Anderson, IN: Warner Press, 1989), no. 289.

Chapter 8

1. Vernon McGee, *Genesis*, Through the Bible Commentary (Pasadena, CA: Thomas Nelson Publishers, 1980), pp. 157–61.

Chapter 10

1. Rex Johnson, *Communication: Key to Your Parents* (Irving, CA: Harvest House, 1978).

Chapter 11

1. Kenneth Prunty, "Elevate the Sunday School through Careful Planning," *Christian Leadership*, April 1982, pp. 1–12.

2. Kenneth Prunty, "Launch a New Church School Year," Annual Sunday School Resource Packet (Anderson, IN: National Board of Christian Education of the Church of God), pp. 1–5.

3.   Donald A. Courtney, "How Teachers Can Increase Their Effectiveness." *Christian Leadership*, April 1982, p. 5.

4.   Ibid., pp. 12–14.

Chapter 15

1.   Dennis Deaton, *Mind Management* (Mesa, AZ: MMI, 1994), pp. 13–14.

2.   Brian P. Hall, *The Personal Discernment Inventory: An Instrument for Spiritual Guides* (New York: Paulist Press, 1980), p. 36.

3.   Simon and Kirchenbaum, *Values Clarification* (New York: Warner Books, Inc., 1995), p. 30.

4.   Carl Jeffery Wright, *God's Vision or Television?* (Chicago: Urban Ministries, Inc., 2004), p. 3.

5.   John Naisbitt, *Megatrends* (New York: Warner, 1984), pp. 11, 18.

Chapter 16

1.   Aubrey Malphurs, *Values-Driven Leadership: Discovering and Developing Your Core Values for Ministry* (Grand Rapids, MI: Baker, 1996), pp. 34, 70–72.

INDEX